Don't Blink

OR YOU'LL MISS IT!

HI MIKE & LOUISE
ENJOY!!!

Bill Hart

Bill Hart

National Library of Canada Cataloguing in Publication Data

```
Hart, Bill, 1930-
  Don't blink-- or you'll miss it!



   ISBN 1-55212-790-7

   I. Title.
PS8565.A6644D66 2001        C813'.6          C2001-910825-7
PR9199.4.H38D66 2001
```

TRAFFORD

This book was published *on-demand* in cooperation with Trafford Publishing.
On-demand publishing is a unique process and service of making a book available for retail sale to the public taking advantage of on-demand manufacturing and Internet marketing.
On-demand publishing includes promotions, retail sales, manufacturing, order fulfilment, accounting and collecting royalties on behalf of the author.

Suite 6E, 2333 Government St., Victoria, B.C. V8T 4P4, CANADA
Phone   250-383-6864   Toll-free   1-888-232-4444 (Canada & US)
Fax   250-383-6804   E-mail   sales@trafford.com
Web site   www.trafford.com   TRAFFORD PUBLISHING IS A DIVISION OF TRAFFORD HOLDINGS LTD.
Trafford Catalogue #01-0190   www.trafford.com/robots/01-0190.html

10   9   8   7   6   5   4   3

INDEX

INDEX

ART WORK BY THE AUTHOR
(ART BY HART)
(Sorry, couldn't resist that!)

CHAPTER 1
THE RAKE IS QUICKER THAN THE FIST

My father was a small, wiry man, as temperamental as an arthritic wart hog with a severe case of adenoids. He clearly understood his own vital importance in the overall scheme of human endeavor and was immovable in his beliefs.

Raised by two old maid aunts in haughty, middle class Victorian England, he was a zealous participant in the well structured and closely ordered British society. Upon arriving on Vancouver Island as an adventurous young man early in the twentieth century, he was appalled to discover he'd joined a society with about as much structure and order as a gun fight in a frontier saloon.

This untidy environment failed to discourage him, however, for, having been well trained in British public schools, he was always ready to demonstrate the advantages of a well structured and orderly society with the aid of a pair of very quick and skilled fists. These, plus a consistently truculent attitude, well fortified with a quick and vile temper, helped him cope with the fact that life

CHAPTER 1
THE RAKE IS QUICKER THAN THE FIST

was, first and foremost, an enemy to be subdued.

To the uninitiated, his volcanic temper was truly a dazzling thing to behold. God help anyone caught within grabbing distance when it erupted. It wasn't that he had a very short fuse. His fuse was nonexistent.

Fortunately for most innocent bystanders, he was able to vanquish the majority of his antagonists with careful, unassailable logic. When logic failed, he would hunch his shoulders, withdrawing his head much like a turtle and glare menacingly at his opponent. Flaring his nostrils, his jaw working as he chewed on his thoughts, he would suddenly exhale through his nose with a terrifying whoosh like an over stressed steam boiler. Turning up the volume of his basso profundo voice to an intimidating level, he would succinctly restate his case. Should his adversary

3

CHAPTER 1
THE RAKE IS QUICKER THAN THE FIST

still not accept the faultless wisdom in my father's point of view, he would be haughtily dismissed as my father walked away.

If, lacking any native sense of self preservation, the blithering fool were to follow my father and continue to doggedly insist that his half-witted opinion had merit, he now faced the distinct danger of having his ill advised beliefs physically removed.

One evening after dinner, Father mumbled something about having left his smoking pipe where he had been working in the garden. As he had a few hundred yards to go, he donned his heavy winter coat and trudged off into the inky darkness to retrieve his beloved pipe. As he entered the garden, he tripped on a clump of grass and stumbled. While regaining his balance, he stepped heavily on the tines of a garden rake

4

CHAPTER 1
THE RAKE IS QUICKER THAN THE FIST

that one of us children had carelessly left lying on the path. When he trod on the rake, the handle flipped up, whacking him enthusiastically on the back before disappearing again into the darkness. Instantly assuming that he was being set upon, probably by Ukrainians, he whirled around, raised his fists in the style of Gentleman Jim Corbet and, bobbing and weaving, stepped heavily on the rake a second time. The rake, probably French, swiftly retaliating for such ill treatment and flung its handle skillfully between his ready fists and smacked him a right good wallop in the mouth. Even from the insularity of the kitchen a few hundred yards away, we clearly heard the outraged bellow that rent the still night air.

I never figured out how my 5'4", 125 pound father could wreak such devastation with his bare

CHAPTER 1
THE RAKE IS QUICKER THAN THE FIST

hands upon something as physically rugged as a hardwood rake handle. Large splinters of it kept surfacing all over the garden for years. In fact, as children, when our reluctant participation in the success of the family plot was required, we would surreptitiously extract the bits of smashed rake from the debris and rebury them in the soil.

None of us could keep a straight face long enough to ask him to explain the inexhaustible supply of bits of broken rake handle.

I still wasn't brave enough to laugh out loud when in my twenties, he laughingly related the sequence of events from that evening of many years before.

CHAPTER 2
BEN SORT OF BUILDS A GO CART

I think Ben probably arrived in this world with one hand full of wrenches and a can of axle grease in the other.

CHAPTER 2
BEN SORT OF BUILDS A GO CART

He wasn't the type to merely tolerate life as it arrived. He rushed wildly to meet it, arms akimbo in welcome and with anticipation. He attacked life with the unshakeable conviction that everything on the face of the earth was either renewable, repairable or renegotiable. At the age of five, while inquisitively poking around in the guts of an ancient alarm clock, he nearly lost a finger when the mainspring suddenly struck at him like an enraged Cobra. When he was ten he hotted up his two wheeler and was at least two lengths ahead of the competition when the sprung front forks (his own invention) collapsed and he left his prominent overbite stuck in the pavement.

A pivotal day in Ben's life occurred one Sunday afternoon in the supermarket parking lot

CHAPTER 2
BEN SORT OF BUILDS A GO CART

when he was introduced to and nearly flattened by a ripping, snarling, tearing little four wheeled screamer called a "Go Cart". He was stunned into rare silence as he watched the diminutive machines only slightly larger than their drivers, rocketing around a temporary race track whose outline was loosely defined by a few scattered hay bales. He decided then and there that he had discovered his life's work; a cause to live for; something he could work towards for the rest of his life; or until something more interesting showed up.   Someday Ben would come to realize that he could have avoided a variety of life's painful scars, physical, emotional and monetary had he just gone out and paid hard cash for whatever it was that caught his interest instead of always building and sometimes even reinventing whatever took his fancy.

But that was just not the way that Ben did things. After having spent at least four minutes inspecting the diminutive beast, Ben, characteristically, figured that it wouldn't be difficult to improve on the breed. A liberal application of his own particular brand of inspired planning would work wonders. A little tweak here would increase the power and a twist there that would surely improve the steering.

Ben actually had once done a little welding and he'd helped a friend assemble a dirt track racer. What else was there to know? He was to soon find out. He started off by liberating an ancient but little used chain saw engine from the town dump. It was a big, scary two cycle Mercury air cooled twin cylinder with

10

CHAPTER 2
BEN SORT OF BUILDS A GO CART

strong anti-social tendencies, a condition that possibly had more than a little to do with why it was reposing on the town dump.

He found that it ran well. Full throttle engendered an exhaust note like rolling thunder and produced enough brute torque to stretch the tracks on an army tank. Even at half speed, it could slather more horsepower onto the pavement than Ben would ever know how to tame.

A few weeks passed and Ben's new toy was ready for a road test. He'd welded up the basic frame from one inch square steel tubing and had bolted on most of the other parts fairly close to where they should have been. He had craftily arranged to have a wheel sticking handily out of each corner and another sticking up to

11

steer with. He snugged the engine down behind the single seat.

His welds were rough and spattery and many of the joints were incomplete. None of the nuts and bolts could boast such modern refinements as lock washers or cotter pins. The wheels didn't match each other in size and Ben hadn't noticed that the rivets in the hub of the steering wheel were loose.

No matter! He proudly pushed his creation out of the basement and onto the driveway where it gleamed deceptively in the Sunday afternoon sun. Without benefit of permit or license, he'd decided to sneak his pride and joy out for just a few short illegal test runs on the public back roads. He expected that some minor adjustments might eventually be necessary but

CHAPTER 2
BEN SORT OF BUILDS A GO CART

certainly nothing serious would crop up! No Way!
In fact, if everything went as well as he pictured it,
he would be ready to compete next week at the
Supermarket races.

After giving the cart a cursory once over he
applied a touch of choke, placed his foot on the
back axle to steady it and gave a mighty pull on
the starter rope.

The big Merc' lit up instantly with a
menacing, primeval snarl, belching flame and
clouds of blue smoke from the vertical exhaust
stacks. Ben pulled his cap around backwards
like a modern Barney Oldfield, plopped himself
down into the driver's seat and without benefit of
helmet, seat belt or even further ado, pressed
lightly on the throttle and vanished down the
street as if attached to the end of a very strong

bungee cord.

Ben had never driven a Go Cart before this day and his lack of experience became immediately self-evident. It hadn't occurred to him that a machine this small with an engine that big might call for a level of skill somewhat exceeding that which he required to herd his old pick-up around town. He was quite awed and more than a little intimidated by the gut wrenching acceleration and the remarkable speed with which the local scenery was whistling by. He'd gone only a couple of hundred yards towards the Riverside Fairgrounds when it became obvious that he'd better soon come up with a plan to negotiate the rapidly approaching abrupt left turn at the bottom of the hill. Gently applying the brakes produced nothing more than a strong whiff

CHAPTER 2
BEN SORT OF BUILDS A GO CART

of burning rubber and the faint impression that the cart was actually accelerating. With the corner approaching at an alarming rate of knots, he abandoned any attempt at finesse and determinedly stamped down on the brakes as hard as he could. For a moment it seemed the machine might be about to slow down when he felt a slight tug on the steering wheel. Next there was a horrendous tearing, scraping sound as though something significant had broken loose and was now dragging along the pavement behind him.

He was just thinking to himself that the brakes might be needing something more than mere adjusting when out of the corner of his eye he noticed the engine, with the back wheels still attached, rumbling proudly along beside him, still

CHAPTER 2
BEN SORT OF BUILDS A GO CART

belching fire and smoke and apparently delighted to make a race of it. He was wondering if there was anything he could do to remedy this untimely turn of events when the engine made an abrupt turn to starboard, executed a very graceful somersault, leapt about thirty feet in the air and trailing a plume of blue smoke, vanished over a roadside hedge. It landed with a tremendous whump right beside the astonished Biddy McCaulay as she was hoeing a row of carrots in her garden. It lay half buried in the soft black earth, now silent except for a steady, apologetic hiss as it cooled down. Biddy, hissing even louder and certainly not apologetically, hammered it into submission with her hoe, applying a skill and dedication never enjoyed by her carrots. She quickly beat the engine to an oily pulp.

16

CHAPTER 2
BEN SORT OF BUILDS A GO CART

Biddy was never quite the same. In fact, the neighbors said, Biddy had never been quite the same since suffering a bout of scarlet fever as a child.

She could hear Ben and the cart continuing on down the hill sounding like a truckload of scrap iron tumbling down a stair well.

Ben hadn't felt it necessary to install any front wheel brakes on his cart mainly because he had no idea the thing would go anywhere near as fast as it did. Anyway, brakes wouldn't have been much help now. He was too busy trying to keep his pile of debris from deserting the road and attacking one of the large, healthy trees that lined the edge.

At this point, things started to happen in bunches. The steering wheel came off in his

17

hands as the cart swapped ends. Ben couldn't see what was next to arrive, which just happened to be the Jackson's Family Annual Picnic and Clambake.   Ben suddenly arrived, backwards, still going at a pretty good clip, without invitation or warning, followed by a small cloud of bouncing and rolling loose parts.

The grass on the Fairgrounds was lush and green and very slippery as Ben and the cart appeared. Ol'Grampaw Jackson, the Family Patriarch, always stood erect and alert when ever out of doors, like a sentry, ready for "the enemy" whom he suspected might attack at any minute. Ol' Grampaw had served in the First World War and hadn't seen anything resembling a bona fide "enemy" in more than fifty years. But by Gum, he was ready!   He had just shoveled a large spoonful of potato salad into his open mouth when, looking over the edge of his plate he spotted something "furrin" streaking straight towards him.

His eyes flipped wide open in astonishment.

"Boche!", he screeched at the top of his lungs, spraying potato salad everywhere. Boche was a derisive term popularly used in reference to German soldiers during the Great War of 1914-'18. As Ben approached, Ol'Grampaw leaned slightly to starboard, adroitly hoisted one spindly leg into the air like a stork and allowed Ben just enough room to whistle underneath. In a final act of treachery, the cart snagged the loaded tablecloth, scattering food and Jacksons in all directions. It then turned a second one

CHAPTER 2
BEN SORT OF BUILDS A GO CART

hundred eighty degrees and with Ben still hanging
to whatever was left, and with the table cloth
flapping in the slipstream, disappeared over the
riverbank with undiminished speed and splashed
into the murky water.

For the first few seconds, nobody moved.
The silence was finally broken by Ol' Grampaw,
shading his eyes and peering suspiciously up the
hill from whence came the "enemy".

"Dang," he grumbled, "I knew I shoulda
brought my rifle!"

They fished Ben out of the river, stunned,
waterlogged, but in not too bad shape despite a
painful road burn on his other end. As he lay on
his back, recuperating, Biddy steamed into view,
obviously overflowing with outrage and looking
more like the Dragon than St. George. She

CHAPTER 2
BEN SORT OF BUILDS A GO CART

reached through the crowd surrounding the supine Ben and was giving him a good old what-for with her hoe handle when she felt Grampaw's hand groping up the back of her skirt, busily doing things that would intimate they were much closer friends than was actually the case. She instantly forgot all about Ben and satisfied her intense pique by harpooning 'Ol Grampaw several times instead.

In a few days the whole kerfuffle was forgotten. By all except Grampaw, that is. He oiled up his rifle and stood guard on the river bank for the rest of the summer. If the "Boche" were about to try for a rematch, he figured to get in a shot or two as they went by. He didn't understand that what he'd seen was merely Ben, sitting on the grass, going backwards at about fifty miles an hour.

They never did find the cart; or the table cloth. And I'll give you five to one that the big Mercury is still buried in Biddie's garden.

He was, as Jersey Bulls are judged, little more than a runt. A purebred, hardly any bigger than a Shetland Pony, he was mostly brown and white with a few splotches of black. He was also very alert, enthusiastic and lightning fast. So

CHAPTER 3
A LITTLE BULL GOES A LONG WAY

small that he required the bovine version of a foot stool to loft him to the altitude necessary to perform the begetting duties which were expected of him.

Jersey bulls are renowned for their consistent truculence and expert use of treachery as far as humankind is concerned. It's a wise farmer who never trusts a Jersey bull until after he's been skinned, butchered and fast frozen. Their favourite hobby is tossing things up in the air and bringing them home impaled on their horns. They particularly dislike bric-a-brac like outhouses or barrels or people or what ever else they manage to overtake. Their social self assessment depends on how long they go without a soul satisfying murder or two and thus more virulence they store up for the next opportunity that might arise.

24

CHAPTER 3
A LITTLE BULL GOES A LONG WAY

Our bull, named "Bill" as many bulls seem to be called, lived inside a very strongly built yard and was never let beyond its confines. In one corner was a doorway leading to a small shed attached to the main barn, thus offering shelter. Like most large barnyard quadrupeds, he never understood the concept of "shelter" and could often be seen standing in the pouring rain or snow storm with only his head inside the building.

I felt sorry for this personable character who would stand peacefully with his head next to the palisade where I could reach through and give him a scratch behind the ear. It had occurred to me that were I restricted to such a boring environment, I would also tend to be a mite churlish.

In the corner of his yard was a section of log that he loved to "fight". He was remarkably skilled at balancing it on the top of his head where he could toss it up high in the air then whip around and thump the daylights out of it as it came down. I decided to assemble a more "high tech" means of amusement for him

Consequently, I retrieved a meter long section of log from the forest, bolted a few feet of logging chain to the centre of one end and craftily attached it with the aid of a large lag screw to hang pendulously from the ceiling of his boudoir. In order to carry out this procedure without becoming a toy myself, I left the shed door closed while he sniffed suspiciously around outside. The log cleared the floor by about a half a meter. The slightest breeze would stir it to swaying. When I opened the door and gave him access, his attention was riveted on this new foreigner, tantalizingly moving slowly from side to side in a

26

most provocative manner, right there inside his very own personal facilities. The nerve!

Bill was a very cool but prickly dude. He wandered over to the doorway and peered disdainfully inside at this cheeky new addition. After standing there for several minutes, just "hanging out", he finally entered far enough to enable him to lean cautiously forward and spray it with a series of suspicious, snot laden sniffs. Very carefully he then proceeded, at glacial speed, until the new toy was hanging next to his right horn. Had anything made a sudden sound or movement just then, he would have gone right out through the roof.

Looking disdainfully superior, he gave it a playful tap. The toy swung a few inches sideways and then returned, giving Bill a polite retaliatory tap on his horn. He recoiled slightly, his eyes

27

opening a little wider than usual, staring at this alien with the suicidal tendency. Its behavior was clearly immoral and possibly even illegal. He gave it a stronger tap and this time it retaliated with a mite more authority. Now he was getting the hang of it. He raised his nose in the air and swung his head away, coolly ignoring his adversary. The next time it gave him a playful knock, he jack-knifed around and belted the log a tremendous crack. The log, having bravely accepted the challenge, swung up in an arc, hit the ceiling with a thump and promptly returned to belt him a harder wallop between his horns than he'd experienced for some years.

Time to regroup! He fled through the doorway with his tail straight up and stood out in his courtyard, watching, his head weaving back and forth, coinciding with oscillations of the log swinging on the end of its tether.

His next foray was made with even more caution. It had become obvious to Bill that this thing was a more dangerous adversary than he'd expected. It took him several minutes to sneak close enough to whack it again. Pretending that he offered nothing but love and gentle kindness, he sidled up to this "provocateur", his attention distant and aloof like a wealthy art connoisseur admiring a painting by Monet in the Louvre. He focused his eyes on a splash of mud on the opposite wall. Without warning, he suddenly wheeled and delivered one, colossal devastating blow and, before vengeance could rear its ugly head, he thundered out into his yard to watch the results from a position of relative safety.

This behavior went on for hours before he figured out that the swinging foreigner had nothing offensive in mind and could be pretty well relied upon to stay where it hung, inside the shed.

This was when his tactics changed. He would stand out in the yard, pawing the ground, moaning professionally, rocking back and forth, working up a head of steam and drawing a bead on his enemy.

Suddenly accelerating across the yard, huffing like a locomotive he would roar through the doorway and nail the impertinent log dead on. Of course, the log, being a beginner at all this and not knowing any better, would swing right up to the ceiling while Bill peered all around to see where it had gone. While his attention was diverted, his foe would enthusiastically return from its excursion and fetch him a tremendous whack somewhere on his person. Tail straight up, he would again wheel around and flee.

CHAPTER 3
A LITTLE BULL GOES A LONG WAY

This simple toy kept Bill busy and on his toes for the rest of the summer. Even late at night the thumping and the moaning could be heard all over the farm as Bill beat the snot out of that chunk of log.

One day in the fall when I came home from school, Bill was gone. He'd been replaced. In his pen was a huge rust colored, Shorthorn bull with no horns at all, short or otherwise and a personality like low-fat yoghurt.

Ah, well, it was nice knowin' you, Kid!

CHAPTER 4
CANOEING TO THE SYMPHONY

The symphony concert, its location and its environs, together, was called "SPLASH 94". At the time, I saw nothing ominous in that designation. Later, I came to ponder if there wasn't a message in it for me.

CHAPTER 4
CANOEING TO THE SYMPHONY

Once a year, on a glorious summer evening, the resident Victoria Symphony Orchestra in the capitol city of British Columbia, the western most province in Canada, performs a free concert.

The orchestra "pit" is an acre or two of barge anchored a few feet offshore from the massive granite causeway that surrounds the harbor in front of the Empress Hotel and the Parliament Buildings. On that 1994 summer evening, by the time the conductor raised his baton to commence the concert, more than eighty thousand lovers of great music, arguably the largest crowd ever to attend a free musical fete anywhere in Canada, had covered every square inch of available dry land or had somehow managed to join the fleet of rowboats, canoes,

CHAPTER 4
CANOEING TO THE SYMPHONY

rafts and even air mattresses floating quietly about in the harbor.

In retrospect and considering everything, it seems, when events come right down to the nub, I'm nothing more than a gullible, hopeless romantic.

Some time previously, while leafing through a glossy travel magazine, I found myself staring at a remarkable color photograph of a stylishly dressed couple reclining in an amply pillowed Venetian Gondola. They were gazing lustfully into each others eyes, lips at the ready, glasses of wine in hand, while a tailed and gowned orchestra sawed and honked away behind them in the misty rays of the setting sun. Wow! It fair took my breath away!

On the next page I came across an

advertisement explaining that the Victoria
Symphony Orchestra would soon perform a
public concert while assembled, somewhat
precariously, I thought, on a barge anchored for
that very purpose in Victoria's inner harbor. As
my eyes scanned the ad, my mind returned to the
couple reclining in the Gondola and putting two
and two together, I started conjuring up a fantasy
in which I envisioned myself ensconced in a
similar Gondola while exchanging erotic glances
with a well-endowed, golden-haired damsel,
preferably prone and even willing. We were
sopping up wine, nibbling delicately on
Camembert and/or ear lobes and exchanging
clever bon mots while the genius of Mozart and
Wagner wafted through the cool evening air. Ah,
the wonder of it all.

35

CHAPTER 4
CANOEING TO THE SYMPHONY

While a pedigreed gondola had never held any position of honor on my want list, I had somewhere acquired a sixteen foot plastic canoe of questionable parentage with "IMA GNU" painted insistently across its bow. This, I thought, could surely serve the same purpose. After all, I had cheese! I had wine! I had large down pillows! I had a paddle! What else could I possible require? Ah, yes! Romance. Of course!

This sort of skullduggery develops much more successfully when at least two or more bodies are striving to reach panting fulfillment.

I had a phone! I knew many desirable women (who could swim)! I dialed. Nope! I dialed again. Nope again! And again. All I heard that I can quote here was two "No Ways" and one "I'd pwobabwy frow up!"

CHAPTER 4
CANOEING TO THE SYMPHONY

The Hell with it! I'll go by myself. I'll show 'em!

I rather suspect that any woman worthy of such a broad classification (no pun intended) possesses a sort of primeval alarm system that goes off should anyone approach bearing disaster in hand.

Alternately, your average blundering male will often happily reach out to greet a disaster like an old friend, then barely survive it, not even aware it's happened and the hoof prints are just another painful memory.

I trundled my collected equipment down to the Songhees waterfront about a mile west of the orchestra barge so I wouldn't have very far to paddle. There was a fitfull wind whipping some very choppy waves directly onto the beach and

37

CHAPTER 4
CANOEING TO THE SYMPHONY

creating conditions which were about to make life more than usually unbearable for this shoe-string gondolier.

I slid "IMA GNU" into the water, loaded in my provisions and prepared to embark.

On a lawn a few feet away sat a little old lady in a well stretched canvas deck chair. Together they exuded an uncanny aura of the Titanic disaster. She was so thoroughly sagged down inside the chair, I wondered if it were possible she could ever escape.

"How clever", I thought to myself. "What a painless way to keep old Grandma from wandering off."

Like a curious gopher she watched my every move, peering at me from between her spindly knees.

CHAPTER 4
CANOEING TO THE SYMPHONY

"Maybe she's putting a hex on me," I chuckled to myself, unsuspecting.

I stepped confidently into my "Gondola" just in time to be assailed by a monstrous rogue wave nearly a foot high which came hissing out of the sunset and bashed us dead amidships.

My ensuing immersion occurred with such speed that I was immobile with surprise. In half a helpless second the canoe was wrong side up. I was too astonished to offer even a token resistance, verbal or otherwise.

In the past I have often defeated stressful situations by slathering the general area with great dollops of sheer will power. Didn't work this time! No such luck! I tried waiting it out in the inverted position, clutching a gunwale in each fist, staring grimly ahead into the murky green depths.

CHAPTER 4
CANOEING TO THE SYMPHONY

Breathing was becoming notably difficult but I thought if I hung in there long enough, kinda quiet like, maybe the darn canoe just might turn right side up again like those Eskimo chaps do.

Nope! I had a sense of watching it all happen to somebody else. I don't know. Maybe I was drowning.

I now realize that since the canoe had spent most of its adult life inverted, I shouldn't have been too surprised that it would wish to instantly and gleefully return to that position, given the slightest hint of an opportunity. Like a stubborn old mule heading back to the barn, there was no retraining it.

I eventually released my grip and surfaced looking like the Monster from Forty Fathoms, handsomely festooned with Victoria Harbor

CHAPTER 4
CANOEING TO THE SYMPHONY

Flotsam and thoroughly smeared with Victoria Harbor Jetsam, though at that moment, the difference had much too fine a point on it to suffer explanation.

It took me a few minutes of heavy gasping to restore my lucidity and figure out which way was up. I then set to and retrieved my cargo which was either drifting resolutely out to sea or had already settled on the bottom.

The little old lady in the deckchair didn't bat an eye. She had boiled the bat wings and sauteed the gnat's kidneys and cackled over the midnight vat. She knew! What was that about a hex? She knew!

I dragged the canoe ashore, emptied out the water and dried out things as best I could. I studiously ignored the covey of onlookers who always seem to materialize out of thin air when ever I start batting my head against fate. I really did feel, though, that their rolling about on the grass, holding their sides and shrieking with laughter was a bit much.

But this descendant of stubborn British stock does not give up easily! Bulldog Grit and all that, donchyano?

I wrung out my "100% Pure Goose Down" pillows, now emanating an odor suspiciously redolent of wet rooster.

Next, in went the water logged snacks, the warm wine and the scummy glasses, though after having been marinated in the depths of Victoria's harbor, there's no way any of that stuff would ever touch these lips. With infinite care I re-stowed the cargo and started to climb aboard a second time.

42

CHAPTER 4
CANOEING TO THE SYMPHONY

A genuine hex laid on with all the magic of the ages has powers beyond the ken of mere mortals. This time I only managed to plant one squishy shoe in the bottom of the IMA GNU when over she went again, taking me head first in a great looping arc. I didn't get time to recite the special epithet that I was prepared to extemporize should this situation ever happen again, which it just had. Once more I was gasping and coughing and bobbing for my goodies.   The shrieks of laughter from the local gentry had tapered off and they were all pointedly staring off in all directions. I'm sure they thought I was attempting to commit suicide or something equally depressing and were studiously ignoring me. Just as well!

Now I realize that this all sounds like I'd

43

never even seen a canoe before, let alone paddled about in one but this is not the case. I was not a complete novice, even with this particular canoe. I had been out many times in "IMA GNU" but never alone. I'd always had company. I always had someone to ride herd on it's other end which was sixteen feet away from me and now, due to the Law of Perversity of Inanimate Objects, had become completely independent of my traditional position of command in the stern.

The problem arose because I had never canoed solo; never just by myself. I had watched with fascination and no little scepticism those TV videos of malnourished northern woodsmen in checkered shirts and floppy hats, paddling expertly along with the canoe tilted over at a

44

paralyzing angle while calmly surfing down what appeared to be Niagara Falls. I noticed the video never included a close-up of the paddlers most assuredly panic stricken face.

Not about to be out smarted by a lump of dumb plastic I dragged the truculent craft onto dry land a second time and started over, from the top!

The little old lady in the deck chair finally spoke up. Solicitously, as though she thought the salt water might have corroded my brain stem, (she's not the first) she enquired,

"Are you alright?"

To which I replied, somewhat petulantly,

"Yes, Thank you. I just need to figure out what I'm doing wrong!"

The whole debacle must have appeared to

her like a scene out of a Buster Keaton movie. With an acute grasp of the obvious, her eyes opened very wide as she soberly offered, "You keep turning that Goddam thing upside down, THAT'S what you're doing wrong!

" ARGGHH!!!

Next to my point of embarkation was a small but sturdy wooden jetty. It had about a foot of clearance between the underside of its deck and the water so I waded in and firmly jammed IMA GNU in that space underneath the wharf's deck.

"Let's see you turn over now," I growled, adding a few personal observations gleaned from my rich, western Canadian verbal heritage. I then again restowed my wine, my wrung out pillows and my mushy cheese and with a dogged sense

CHAPTER 4
CANOEING TO THE SYMPHONY

of do or die I waded ashore, walked back along the wharf, climbed over the side and gingerly lowered myself into the canoe like a broody hen settling onto a clutch of thin-shelled eggs. I had figured that with my weight added to the sodden debris, the canoe would sink just enough to slide out from under the wharf.

Miscalculation! It wouldn't budge. She was well and truly stuck!

At this point I must have become slightly deranged for I can only take so much. In a rage, I lay on my back in the bottom of the canoe, raised my feet up above my head and shoved mightily against the underside of the wharf deck. By simultaneously laying about me with the paddle and lubricating everything within reach with all the filthy epithets that I could remember or

47

invent, the damn thing suddenly popped loose like a champagne cork and came within a whisker of dumping me into the drink for the third time. Thank you for the applause!

Still, considering the situation, it was a pretty good launch, accomplished while I was stretched out in the bottom of the canoe. The ballast must be kept low, y'know.

In the distance I could hear the orchestra tuning up. In order to maintain a low centre of gravity, I remained slumped in the bilge like a Formula One race car driver. Very difficult to paddle from this position but it can be done. Every once in a while I would cautiously raise myself just high enough to peek over the gunwale. By now the scenario had taken on all the appearances of a jailbird escaping from

48

CHAPTER 4
CANOEING TO THE SYMPHONY

Alcatraz in a small garbage scow. Every time I peered over the gunwale I discovered I was going in the wrong direction. More dedication and effort produced considerably more speed, but still in the wrong direction. It was a bit of a shock to discover I simply couldn't go in any other direction but down wind while the concert, naturally, was in the opposite direction and getting more so with each stroke. I tried sitting in the centre and paddling and that didn't work because I couldn't reach enough water. I tried paddling from one end and then the other but still couldn't maintain the proper heading. If I hadn't been fortunate enough to find a hand hold in the stonework under Johnson Street bridge, I could well be writing this from somewhere in Argentina or the Aleutians, depending on the wind direction.

49

CHAPTER 4
CANOEING TO THE SYMPHONY

I eventually discovered that since the bow always pointed down wind regardless of my intention or efforts, I could control the direction (more or less, mostly less) of travel by sitting in the stern and paddling backwards, sort of like prying the rotten thing along by using the paddle as a crowbar.

As I levered my way up-wind past the causeway floats, I crept near an American Melmac yacht not noticeably smaller than Liz II. Relaxing on deck was a ropey old galoot with a large rummy looking drink wrapped in his fist and sucking on the Grandaddy of all Cheroots. Puffing spasmodically, he watched suspiciously as I approached. As I back paddled within earshot he remarked in a rich Yankee drawl,

"Either y'all s'posed to sait in the oather

aind of that thang or yer goin' in the wrong
drection, Haw Haw Haw!".

Finally I got to use that scintillating bon mot
I was telling you about.

"Aw Shaddup"!, I countered brilliantly.

As I backed stubbornly across the harbor
a couple of things became very clear to me. First,
a rear view mirror on a canoe would be a definite
aid to navigation, at least, the way I do it, and the
other was how I now understand why it took so
long to populate western Canada. For the first
three hundred years or so, the poor chaps tried to
do it by canoe. What a cruel joke. I wonder how
many bright faced, eager, ambitious young
settlers slowly paddled backwards into oblivion
because the wind just happened to be blowing

from the wrong direction that month.

"Out west somewhere" was never so far away! As I neared the barge where my fantasy had me sitting back and opening my bottle of wine, I heard the exciting strains of what I recognized as the finale of the 1812 Overture.

Now why couldn't someone have warned me that, as an aid to realism, the great, hairy explosions that punctuate the end of the 1812 Overture would this time be coaxed from strategically placed, real live cannons using real live flashy gunpowder producing huge clouds of real live smoke.

Pointing straight at me, they were. I didn't suspect a thing. As the first bloody great BANG went off in my right ear, I reflexed about three feet straight up and very nearly went into the drink again. The muzzle flashes were extremely close and I discovered that paddling backwards isn't that difficult after all. I guess fate figures it's just as effective to scare a man to death as drown him.

I finally swept into view accompanied by thunderous applause which I hoped was for me but I suspect was meant for the orchestra.

The concert was over.

By this time, the wind, as vagrant as ever, had died entirely as I paddled up along side my friend Dave, who I had planned to meet, as he allowed his powerboat to drift slowly around the harbor. He looked at me in wide eyed astonishment.

"What the Hell happened to you"? he

asked.   "Don't start with me," I grumped back.

I must have looked quite a sight in my summer whites, soaking wet, still festooned in my harbor finery and generously smeared with very old 10W-40 engine oil, sea weed and fish scales.

He kindly took my bow line in hand and towed me back to my starting point.

Another Good Samaritan helped me load the canoe onto the roof of my Van. He kept saying "Excuse me"?   He thought I was addressing him but in fact I was muttering very quietly and very earnestly to the canoe.   It's probably a good thing he couldn't hear what I was saying. I was using words like "axe" and "power saw", stringing them together with epithets one rarely uses at a church garden party and gets to be invited back.

I checked the canvas chair and the little old lady was gone. Probably flitting about in the dark, looking for more gnat's to disembowel.

It took only three days to sell the canoe!

CHAPTER 5
SOMETIMES IT JUST AIN'T WORTH IT

The last woman Herb introduced me to
turned out to be not my type. She was arrogant,

hated men, applied her perfume with a fire hose and her make up with a putty knife. And that was the good stuff. Naturally, when he started to extol the virtues of this latest ethereal vision he had discovered, I started checking ticket prices to the Aleutians. However, Herb's persistent scheming prevailed and the next thing I knew, he was saying,

"I'd like you to meet Ilsa."

She was tall, blonde and blue eyed with an uptown figure and a way of moving it about that instantly transformed the average cool dude like me into a bumbling, tongue tied idiot. It was an indication of her gracious benevolence that in spite of my obvious brain damage, she agreed to go out with me.

My particular form of brain damage is

strictly related to beautiful women. The more beauty, the more damage. When she flashed those gorgeous big blues on me and purred with that Marlene Deitrich accent, my voice tape got stuck on Fast Rewind. There isn't anything in the world that I wouldn't have done for her once I discovered "mein scnibble" (or something that sounded like that,) was her pet name for me. That is, after I started breathing again.

I never enquired, but she must have been in her early forties. A mite young for me, but what the Heck! She told me, in shattered English, about her childhood, about going to school, about coming to Canada several years before from somewhere in Germany. I never did figure out from where.

My weakened knees couldn't believe my

58

CHAPTER 5
SOMETIMES IT JUST AIN'T WORTH IT

incredible good luck when this Goddess agreed to meet me when I suggested we do lunch. I had taken advantage of a fleeting bout of uncharacteristic courage and suggested lunch because I think I'm probably far less threatening around noon than I am closer to bed time. During our lunch I had another brief infusion of nerve and suggested that we go out for dinner sometime. Holy doodle, she accepted!

A couple of days later during dinner I enquired about her marital status.

"Yah, Yah," she oozed, "ischt ben zingle am." Well, now, that's a load off my mind. Nothing quite as unraveling as testy husbands that pop up like targets in a shooting gallery. Now if I can just get my mouth to stop hanging open like the back door on my long johns.

CHAPTER 5
SOMETIMES IT JUST AIN'T WORTH IT

As we drove around that evening after dinner she seductively suggested that I come up to her sixth floor apartment for a nightcap.

As I was still having a dreadful time trying to unravel her English, I didn't believe what I thought I'd heard. I hoped that she was being bowled over by the sophisticated accent on my gibberish but I suspect she figured that inviting me up to her apartment was the only way she'd ever get within a parsec of her home again.

After I inveigled her into rephrasing it several times, I was finally convinced.

"Yep, we're going up to her place," I crowed to myself. With that, my mind took off on a trip of erotic conjecture and left the rest of me behind to fend for myself. When it returned moments later it had fully planned the next

CHAPTER 5
SOMETIMES IT JUST AIN'T WORTH IT

hundred years, leaving nothing out.

A solitary housefly droned over us as we were sat together on her couch, sipping something exotic and discussing two entirely different subjects because neither of us could understand what the heck the other one was going on about when her door buzzer sounded from the main entrance, six stories below.

"Himmel" she says, frowning.

"Aw Nuts!" I says to myself.

She turned towards me as she hung up the phone connected to the lobby.

"Ischt mein husband" she says, obviously delighted.

"Himmel" I says, and check out the street below for a passing ladder truck.

"I thought you said you're zingle," I

squeeked.

"Yah, Yah, Zince tree weeks I'm zingle ben. Now comen home mein husband, no more, ischt nein ben zingle."

I wasn't listening. I was trying to formulate a survival plan and decide how loud I was going beg when Ilsa opens the door and in walks the biggest, toughest, coolest looking guy I've ever seen.

Ilsa introduced us.

"Beel, Franz dis my husband ischt"!

My stomach was convulsing and I was shaking too much to even get up off the couch. I couldn't even say anything comprehensible. My mind, that part of me that forms words, was so guilt ridden by all its erotic plans involving Ilsa with chandeliers and paint brushes and

CHAPTER 5
SOMETIMES IT JUST AIN'T WORTH IT

Cointreau, that it had seized up entirely.

Burbling like a ten gallon coffee urn, I offered my hand, expecting it to be surgically removed.

Franz was completely disarming and spoke flawless English. It was as though we were old buddies. According to rules of chivalry prevalent when I was brought up, he should have been punting me off the balcony right about now. He just smiled and enquired about my rapidly diminishing well being while I continued to gurgle incomprehensibly. He asked me, while patting me on the shoulder, if I'd had any success in making love to Ilsa.

"With Ilsa," he winked, "you really have to fight for it."

I nearly had a fit. There were little

explosions going off all over my body as my overloaded synapses shorted out. I remember thinking that whatever my reply, the next thing to drone over me wouldn't be that blasted house fly, it'd be the last rites. I managed to dredge up enough courage to set my jaw, look him directly in the eye and reply, "Burtzanglesnurb." and in case that wasn't sufficient, I frowned and forcefully threw in, "Mertz!".

Ilsa was chattering away in German at the kitchen table. Franz was dividing his attention between us. I was insinuating my still pristine body towards the exit. When Franz turned away from me to pay some attention to Ilsa (and who could blame him?) I whipped open the front door, shouted, "Sorrygottagobyebyeseeya," and hit the stairs flat out. I didn't have time to wait for an

CHAPTER 5
SOMETIMES IT JUST AIN'T WORTH IT

elevator.

I only saw Ilsa once again. One sunny morning I spotted her sashaying along the sidewalk in my direction. Part of me was panting for a rematch, but my mind, that other part of me that harbours a strong desire for survival, led me by my sweaty hand into a doorway and up a flight of stairs, where I stayed until the coast was clear.

Sometimes, but only sometimes, it isn't worth it.

CHAPTER 6
MY FIRST REAL GHOST

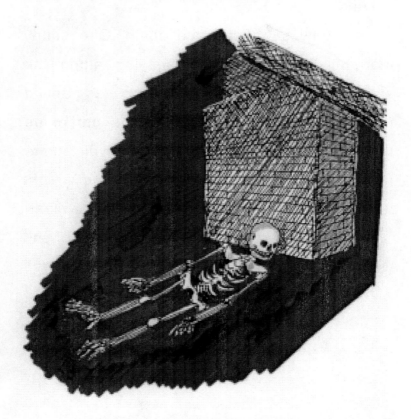

At the tender age of about seven years I
lived with my parents and various other transient

relatives in a rather seedy but ornate 1880s Victorian Mansion. It was one of these places that was obviously an experiment in architecture which, I suspect, was intended to exude a rather grandiose air but wasn't quite able to pull it off. The layout of the rooms and interconnecting passages made no sense at all. The ceilings were so high they developed their own weather patterns with the occasional storm front creeping from room to room. The place was so big it was only marginally better than living out of doors.

The huge attic, the precise location of this singular experience, was more of a loft than anything else. A cobwebbed, dim place, it was lit only by the occasional hanging light bulb and a pokey window in each gable end. While most attics today are not big enough to be finished in any way, this old attic was at least completely floored with edge grain fir and almost ready to move in. Some of the local kids used it as a roller rink.

It was while we lived in this house that I experienced the first genuine nightmare of my young life. Some sixty plus years later I can still see clearly in my mind's eye a large, pale yellow skeleton lying on its back on the attic floor with its grinning skull propped up at an angle, completely hidden behind the immense red brick chimney that ran from the basement through each floor and up through the roof. I once spent quite a bit of time in that attic but after that realistic nightmare, I only once ever went up there again.

About a year after experiencing that scary dream, my parents announced that we were

CHAPTER 6
MY FIRST REAL GHOST

about to move to a new location. I knew instinctively that I couldn't walk away and leave this ghost business as it presently was. I wrestled with the conviction that I must beard my personal lion in his dusty den. I thought about it a lot and almost came to the conclusion that the likely hood that a real skeleton reposed undiscovered behind the chimney was indeed, very thin. However, every time I seriously considered the long climb up the stairs followed by even a fleeting glance to make absolutely sure that my nemesis didn't really exist, the green wobblies turned my guts to mush and I would put off the day of reckoning, to be handled another time.

Finally, when everyone in the family was busy, sorting stuff out and packing things in boxes I knew the day of relocation was rapidly approaching and I could delay no longer. Taking my courage in both hands, for that was what it required, I crept silently up the dark, varnished, gloomy stairway to the attic. Creeping silently up a dark stairway in an ancient Victorian Mansion was a good trick that I couldn't duplicate today. In those days I weighed not much more than a feather or two. My present weight would cause every board in the place to screech in outrage.

I silently tiptoed closer and closer to the chimney behind which lay the worm that constantly gnawed at my courage. Suddenly I realized I had ceased to breathe. At the same time I also realized that a complete circumnavigation of the chimney had now become technically necessary in order to completely exorcize the image from my mind. If indeed there was a skeleton hiding behind that red brick flue, I had no intention of giving it the opportunity

70

to latch onto me as I roared past. Forcing my lungs into action, I let out a very loud blood curdling screech, shot completely around the chimney, made a beeline for the top of the stairs and without hardly touching a single step, disappeared from view.

Under the fearful pressure of the possibility of actually meeting face to bony face with my imaginary demon, I hadn't noticed my father sitting quietly on a box, going through some papers by the dim light of the small window in the gable end. The first inkling he had that he wasn't completely alone was a screaming, banshee howl, as he described later, "like a speeding car locking up all four wheels on dry pavement". His immediate reaction was to throw all his papers high into the air, make a loud "Whuff" like a startled bloodhound and try very hard to beat me to the bottom of the stairs. He might have accomplished this small ambition if I had only realized it was only he who

CHAPTER 6
MY FIRST REAL GHOST

was after   me but all I heard was unidentified
footsteps gaining on me in the gloom. As I felt the
sounds getting closer I was sure that my ghost must
have relocated his hiding place and now at full speed,
was about to place his bony hand on my shoulder. I
shifted into overdrive, wet my pants and disappeared
like a puff of smoke. Now truly in full flight, I had
reached that cosmic state where I was no longer
attached to my body, where I seemed to be able to
attain any speed I wished. I certainly wasn't about to
let that most horrible of demons grab hold of me.

As my pursuer, my father didn't stand a
chance. I think he would have killed me if I hadn't
made myself scarce while his nerves settled down
and he pulled himself together. He was as jumpy as
a dyspeptic cat for several days. Whenever I came
into a room where he was, he would silently peer at
me over his spectacles with gimlet eye, trying to figure

just what the Hell I thought I was doing up in the attic at that particular time and I never had nerve enough to tell him

Apparently, as it turned out, he would never go into the attic again, at least without first ascertaining my whereabouts.

I don't blame him. I never went up into that blasted attic again either, ghost or no ghost

CHAPTER 7
DOGS ARE JUST FURRY PEOPLE

Dogs are such neat fellas. They ramble through life acting as though they know they're only for here for short time and they'd rather not be confronted by anything that might require serious concentration or smacks of any degree of confusion. In fact, I know of only three things that cause dogs to really focus their intellect. Food is one. An alien neighbourhood mutt ranks up there with food, but cats are the overpowering third. Confront the average dog with food and you've got some of his attention. A second, unknown dog stumbling onto the scene will raise his interest and sometimes overload his olfactory equipment even more, but leave a cat lying around or even anything that looks like a cat and you've got his riveted devotion.

I was having my auto fueled up at the local station when a small, nondescript mutt of undefinable parentage came hurrying along the side walk. I could tell from the glassy look in his eyes that he had nothing important on his mind (as usual) and probably couldn't even remember where he was going but wherever it was, it required hurrying. As he went by I laid my cat sound on him.

My cat sound is a trick I do with my lips that produces the exact "mew" of a small kitten. Attributable to a narrow gap between my front teeth, it's something I learned to do while I was still quite

small and over the years it's been a source of great hilarity to me and a source of intense frustration to several generations of dogs and one frustrated Father.

I would wait until my Father was nodding off at the head of the table after dinner and I would "mew". He would immediately go nuts.

"How'd that cat get in the house"? he'd

roar, "Who let that cat in"?

I'd go to the door, open it and pretend to usher the "cat" out side. Peace would prevail for about five minutes or so and just as he would start to doze off, I'd do it again. His reaction was always the same. Roaring outrage! I'd get up again and let the "cat out" and peace would return.

And so it went.

On this particular day my cat sound must of successfully interrupted a particular thought that was attempting to become legitimate in his dog brain for he stopped dead in his tracks like he'd been quick frozen. I could almost see him thinking.

"There's cat heresabouts", he commented dourly to himself while looking carefully all in all

CHAPTER 7
DOGS ARE JUST FURRY PEOPLE

directions. I made the sound again. Ignoring me, he stood on his hind legs and looked into my auto, first from one side, then the other, being careful not to mess up the paint job.

"Nope"------"Nuthin".

He sat and had a dedicated scratch while the puzzle lurched about in his mind. He stared intently at the car.

"Mebbe underneath"!

He crawled part way underneath the machine, looking carefully about. He came back out and checked out the interior again

I mewed again.

"There, I heard it again", he thought, checking the whole area around the pump island and the shop doorway. Then he again stood on his hind legs like an aspiring preacher and

CHAPTER 7
DOGS ARE JUST FURRY PEOPLE

peered up and down the street in both directions. He was wonderfully confused. As soon as he started to lose interest, I would mew again.

At this point he spotted a thick privet hedge directly across the road which focused his attention and he stared at it intently for a few moments before deciding that the missing cat was obviously behind that hedge. No longer confused, he assumed his decision must be the correct one and streaked off across the road to dismember the cowardly cat obviously hiding behind that hedge.

In his passage across the street, he almost ran smack into the front of Mrs. Harley's passing Vauxhall causing her to lean on the brakes with such dedication that she nearly came out through the windshield. I wonder where Mrs. Harley

CHAPTER 7
DOGS ARE JUST FURRY PEOPLE

learned language like that.

It was at this point that things really got out of hand. Just as the speeding mutt arrived at the end of the hedge, the biggest cat I'd ever seen stepped confidently out right into his path. It was jet black and shiny and obviously closely related to a Panther and had just enough time to turn its astonished head to admire his arriving adversary when he got "T boned". The dog, taken completely by surprise, hit the cat dead amidships at flank speed and bowled it over several times. Just before he got to the cat, when he realized that a collision was unavoidable he slammed on the binders and started caterwauling at the top of his lungs. I'll bet his life flashed before his eyes several times when that monster cat popped into view. While he did have the cat at a decided disadvantage for a second or two, he wisely failed to press his momentary supremacy and wasted no time in disentangling himself. He then continued on his journey, going flat out in a straight line away from the cat, warning all bystanders of his coming in as loud a voice as possible.

The cat, having been converted from a real cool pussy dude to a nervous wreck dude in a couple of milliseconds, continued to spit and roar and roll about in the dust for quite a while after it's nemesis has faded from view. It had resorted to fighting with itself for a defensive moment or two before strutting spastically on its jittery way, peering in all directions, spitting occasionally and obviously very wary about what evil, noisy missile was going to collide with him next and

81

CHAPTER 7
DOGS ARE JUST FURRY PEOPLE

from which direction.

The chap feeding my gas tank at no time noticed anything out of the ordinary. He just wondered why I was hanging over the fender, laughing like an idiot.

CHAPTER 8
FRED TRIES SURFING

It was early in the winter. Small patches of snow lay on the ground. Lots of mud. Cold and damp.

CHAPTER 8
FRED TRIES SURFING

I was working as a farm implement service representative and winter is the time of year when sensible farmers call on me and my ilk to come and monkeywrench their equipment in readiness for spring. I say sensible because some farmers don't schedule their equipment service until the day they need to use it. One brilliant chap called me out to service his baler one warm morning in June when he discovered it wouldn't bale. It didn't take long to uncover the rock hard maple tree stump he'd tried to bale the previous summer which had wrecked his machine and which he'd forgotten about.

I arrived at Fred's farm in the early darkness of the evening. He offered to feed me supper but I had considered this possibility so had eaten on the way there. Fred was a typical smelly old bachelor farmer. His kitchen was lighted by a single anemic light bulb hanging down from the centre of the ceiling. The only way to get his house even reasonably clean would be to burn it down.

He explained the ins and outs of how his tractor was giving him trouble so I headed for the tool shed to see what was up.

Fred must have eaten his dinner with some speed for he materialized beside me just a few moments after I started to work.

He was a friendly, talkative chap. He told me how he came out from England in 1919 as a veteran from the First World War and settled on the farm that he still occupied. He watched me for a few moments while I took things apart and peered into the tractor's oily interior. He told me about being in the trenches during the first war.

As we spoke I was suddenly shocked almost into a panic when the dark shed lit up like someone had fired off a magnesium flare in the doorway. I turned to look for the source of this brilliance and spotted, a short distance away, two incredibly bright lights speeding straight towards me at about ground level. It wasn't until then that I noticed that the building we were in was situated precisely off the end of the main runway of the biggest airport in the area. The two bright lights were attached to what had developed into a very large, noisy aircraft which at that moment was obviously intending to fly through the doorway and join us.

Old Fred nearly fell over with laughter as he watched me sprinting of into the darkness.

CHAPTER 8
FRED TRIES SURFING

"Never had one crash here yet!" he roared with his English accent that sounded like his mother must have been frightened by a buzz saw.

This experience happened not long after the Cuban Missile Crisis when everyone was still pretty jumpy and somewhat concerned that they might not be around to greet the next dawn. It occurred to me that the particular location of Fred's farm didn't leave much room for survival should the serious shooting begin.

I had not fallen for the official propaganda concerning the safety of fall out shelters. The Canadian Prime Minister announced that in case of a nuclear attack, he would be found in his fall out shelter. I could only wonder who would find him.

CHAPTER 8
FRED TRIES SURFING

I knew, without being told, that large airfields would be one of the first targets, especially the big one next to Fred's farm. Without trying to sound like an alarmist I pointed out to him the tenuous location of his home, what with radiation and fall out and all that, not to mention that a hydrogen bomb exploding less than a mile away would tend to mess up his organization.

"Aw, all that talk about fallout 'll never bother me," he buzzed in his deep voice, "if I 'ave a problem I'll just go see the M.O.".

"The M.O."? I squeeked, still vibrating from that close call with an obviously over loaded aircraft.

"What's an M.O."? I asked. Maybe he knows something I don't, I thought to myself.

CHAPTER 8
FRED TRIES SURFING

"The Medical Officer", he sneered, relegating me to the rank of a pimple faced rookie who hadn't ever heard of an "M.O." Then I remembered my father telling me about his scary experiences with the "M.O" during the first world war.

Fred displayed such comfortable, rock solid, immovable faith in the talents of his M.O. that I began to wish I could adopt some similar guru on which to dote and thus avoid all the stress and strain brought about by the fear of instant combustion. After listening to my father describe the miserable success rate of his M.O. during WW1, I knew it would never work for me.

Soon he announced that he had some chores to do and disappeared off into the darkness. He hadn't been gone long before I

CHAPTER 8
FRED TRIES SURFING

heard a faint shout for help. It seemed so far away that I ignored it at first. I really wanted to get the job finished and be off home.

The shouts persisted so I resigned myself to becoming involved in some sort of time wasting diversion and started to look around to find the source of the cries.

I soon located Fred in a dimly lit shed some distance away. He was standing tethered to a very relaxed horizontal heifer who was, as far as I could tell, stone cold dead. He had one end of a stout rope wrapped several times around his wrist. The other end was looped around the neck of the corpse. I concluded, from the evidence, that he expected me to assist him in manhandling the remains out into the yard to be later disposed of with the aid of the tractor.

CHAPTER 8
FRED TRIES SURFING

"Give the auld bitch a good boot will you whilez I pullz on the rope."

I eyed the corpse as I walked over to it. There was absolutely no sign of life. There was no way this animal was about to move under her own steam. I hauled off and gave her a kick on the rump.

"Put your back into it," he scolded.

I calculated that the next kick I applied should at least loft the beast right out through the doorway. It didn't even move.

I was only just warming to the task and had applied several more persuaders when the "corpse" suddenly sprang to life. With a loud "Baw" of protest she leapt nimbly to her feet and shot out into the darkness towing Fred adroitly along like a water skier. Her rapid acceleration

CHAPTER 8
FRED TRIES SURFING

was aided by a skillfully directed jet of liquid feces, the majority of which hosed me generously from top to bottom. Fred attempted to dig in his heels to slow her down but the animal was in her prime and he couldn't keep his feet under him for more than a second or two when he fell face down onto the manure covered floor. With the rope wrapped around his wrist, he couldn't have released the heifer if he had wanted to and he surfed off, nose down, at high speed into the darkness. I can tell you that he didn't go quietly either.

It was some time before he returned to thank me for my assistance. I was still swabbing myself down with handfuls of hay and mumbling to myself about getting a job as a brain surgeon while he seemed to be generally unconcerned, as though this sort of thing happened every day.

I thought I looked horrible enough but next to him I was ready for the Governor's Ball. He was certainly a rare sight to behold. He had lost both of his rubber boots which were mired somewhere out in the darkened barnyard. He was slathered from head to toe with a grisly mixture of mud, grass, old hay and manure. He had also collected a number of bloody cuts and abrasions, reminiscent of someone who'd been dragged reluctantly but speedily through a barbed wire fence and needed immediate attention with some bandages or maybe a needle and some thread or maybe a staple gun.

"Aw", he grumbled, "she's a good un, but I usually have to tow her around with the tractor. She's just a bit bloody minded".

CHAPTER 8
FRED TRIES SURFING

I put on a spurt of speed to get the tractor finished. One more battle like that last one and Fred would be a candidate for a ride in a hearse. He really needed that tractor.

I never again had occasion to return to Fred's farm. I sometimes wonder how he made out. I'm sure he never surrendered.

CHAPTER 9
CHUCK FREE FALLS

     Not far from the back door of our big old farm house was a tall, bushy Douglas Fir tree. It had a trunk as straight as a ship's mast and must have been well over a hundred feet high.

CHAPTER 9
CHUCK FREE FALLS

Its branches, evenly spaced, seemed to have been craftily arranged to obliterate most the view of the farm from our kitchen window.

Chuck, a cousin who lived with us as a family member, overheard my grandmother remark about how nice it would be if some of the branches could be removed from the offending tree. Her remark was made without any gravity, much as one might casually remark that they had heard that there might be rain on Friday, right after lunch.

Chuck figured that if he took up the challenge and trimmed off some of the branches it might be a route to admiration, heroism or even family fame. He "filched" a cross cut saw from my father's shop, detoured to pick up a ladder and headed for the lower branches of the tree. I say "filched" because he required secrecy for had any of the adults got wind of his plans, his game would have been called on

CHAPTER 9
CHUCK FREE FALLS

account of the knack he had cultivated in the past, where he unfailingly managed to bust himself up pretty good and inflict severe damage on the surrounding scenery.

He had, at least, figured out that he would need to start at the top of the tree and work his way down. Maybe it was the thin air up there that eroded what little logic he was utilizing for it didn't include informing him that standing on the very branch that he was so industrially sawing away at next to the trunk might be marginally hazardous.

Suddenly there was a loud crack and as we watched, Chuck vacated the tree in a most efficient and spectacular manner.

I considered it quite admirable of him to arrange to hurtle down that side of the tree with the most branches. As he sailed downwards, he broke off each branch in turn as he connected with it. As he fell, he accumulated beneath himself a thick wad of greenery which acted vaguely like a parachute that both slowed his fall and provided an efficient cushion on which he eventually landed. I rather suspect that had the tree been taller, hence more branches, he might never have reached earth at all but drifted lazily off, over the horizon on a magic carpet of green fuzz.

Not surprisingly, he was yelling at the top of his lungs all the way down, the cracking of the branches providing a sort of rhythmic tattoo.

"Arghhh" SNAP, (grab) "Yeoowww" SNAP, (snatch) "OHfer..." SNAP, (grab) and so on, all the way to ground level.

In spite of his accumulated bedding, he still landed with a fair thump. Sitting up, stunned, looking much like he wasn't sure of his whereabouts, he felt himself all over and decided that he might be still relatively undamaged when the crosscut saw which he had cast aside in his haste suddenly arrived somewhat tardily and fetched him a good clout on the top of his head. Nobody could figure out where it had been in the interim, possibly balanced on a branch somewhere, I suppose.

Nothing bleeds like a superficial head wound and this might have been his only injury had not the kerfuffle attracted the attention of my father who arrived on the scene, his face dark with foreboding. Chuck had spotted him coming across the yard and, no fool he, jumped to his feet and fled, catching the toe of his boot on the top rail of the fence as he broad jumped over it. The resulting face down impact on the other side just spread the blood around a little better and blackened both eyes but failed to deter him from escaping. He again sprang nimbly to his feet and galloped off into the distance.

None of us hung around any longer than

CHAPTER 10
CHUCK FREE FALLS

Chuck once we saw Dad coming. He may have had a question or two for which he would demand answers as to why his favourite saw was laying on top of a pile of freshly pruned branches, a long way from its home on the shop wall. Unfortunately, or fortunately, depending which side of the fence you favoured, there was no one left in the vicinity for him to grill. He picked up his saw and stumped off to his shop, no wiser than he'd ever been about what had actually just taken place.

Dad sported a very short attention span and if any sinner could manage to stay clear of him for a couple of hours after such a mishap, he would forget all about it. Which he did.

We dunked Chuck's head up and down in the horse trough for a while, the cold water seized up every blood vessel north of his Adam's apple and washed away any outward evidence of mishap. Even the muddy look around his eyes almost disappeared.

Several days crept by before any of the family noticed that all the branches from one side of the tree had mysteriously disappeared.

Nobody seemed puzzled by this situation. Nothing was ever said of the matter. I guess nobody was dumb enough to enquire.

Or maybe too smart

CHAPTER 10
MY FIRST CAR

1916 FORD "T"

She was mostly rust. The canvas was hanging down in shreds between the roof bows. The upholstery had completely rotted away leaving only a collection of rusty coil springs and shreds of horsehair. The tires had rotted free years before.

But she was all mine, bought with my first pay cheque at the age of thirteen during the summer of '44.

She had come off the assembly line in 1916 and had obviously done a fair amount of work in her time. Since then had been sitting quietly in the depths of an old barn for nearly twenty years. Just a roost for generations of fat hens, she was patiently waiting for me to show up.

We became instant buddies. She taught me a lot. Not just about things mechanical, but the value of patience, the process of deductive thinking, the need for constant awareness and

103

how to make bandages out of newspaper and electricians tape. And I sure made a lot of them.

Mom drove our Model A pick up and we towed the "T" home on it's rims. On the back roads? Nothing doing! Right down the main highway! Try that today.

It took me ages to get the old bucket to run for the first time. I took the engine all apart, put it all back together again, took it apart again and so on. I don't know what I was looking for. I figured there must be some evil spirit hidden down in the guts somewhere and all I had to do was locate and exorcize it.

As I discovered later, there was no reason for it not to run. Model Ts were remarkably fundamental. There were no hidden nooks and crannies like on a modern engine. There wasn't much to go wrong.

Nowadays, when you pop the hood open on your favourite chariot, you can't even see the engine, there's so much festoonery slathered all over the top of it. And if something goes haywire, too bad. Without enough electronic diagnostic equipment to navigate a missile to the moon there's nothing you can do.

When you lifted the hood on a T, everything was right there in front of you. No complications. No special tune up equipment required. To check the engine oil level, you opened a small tap on the side of the engine. If no oil came out, you opened the second, lower tap. If still no oil came out, you closed the bottom tap and added oil until it ran out of the top tap. That simple! When you bought a Model T, it

105

came with one wrench that would loosen or tighten pretty well anything you needed to loosen or tighten. Mostly tighten.

The first thing to look for were ignition problems. Weak spark could make the engine a little recalcitrant and hard to start. They had a separate coil for each spark plug and each coil had a vibrator on top and they all vibrated sequentially at different notes of the scale. A wonderful sound. The voltage generated by one of these vibrator coils was enough to barbecue a Hereford steer. Many a screwdriver got tossed into infinity when some poor fellow accidentally touched a sparkplug wire while poking about in his T's innards and got spazzed by several thousand aggressive volts.

A Swedish immigrant neighbour showed up

one day when I was working on adjusting the vibrators and admitted that he had "Vunce owned a Model T". In his soft musical accent he went on,

"I yoost to crank dat old bitch until the vater boiled in the radiator before she vould start".

I had reached the point in my ministrations with the T that I didn't bother to put it all back together each time I tore it down, since experience had shown me, it wasn't going to run anyway.

Late one night, I was just dropping off to sleep, when, like receiving a divine revelation directly from the mouth of God, I was suddenly told why I couldn't get it to start.

I quickly got dressed. It was nearly midnight. I lit my lantern, crept out the basement door and went to work on her. In a few moments

CHAPTER 10
MY FIRST CAR

I had analyzed the problem and done the necessary adjustment. Not about to wait until morning to see if my theory was correct, I went through the start up drill and heaved mightily on the crank. She lit up on the first pull with a roar like a WW2 fighter plane.

I hadn't bothered to hook up the exhaust pipe, since it wasn't about to run anyway. Nor had I bothered to put any water in the radiator. I mean, it's not going to run, is it?

My mother flew to the kitchen window when she heard the roar, having no idea I wasn't upstairs asleep. When she saw me gandy-dancing about in the light from the lantern, trying to do fourteen things all at once, she wasn't about to be left out of the fun and promptly rushed out to join me and to offer her services.

CHAPTER 10
MY FIRST CAR

She knew how frustrated I'd been, not able to even get a cough out the wretched old bucket.

"Can I help"? she queried at the top of her lungs, outshouting the roar of the open exhaust.

"Get a bucket of water, quick" I yelled, "and pour it in the radiator".

Old Mumsy could really move it when the mood was on her. She was back in a flash with a bucket of water which she dumped in the radiator. I hadn't bothered to tighten up the radiator hoses either. Why bother, it won't run anyway.

Mumsy kept pouring a steady stream of water in the radiator which ran out as fast as she poured it in. Every couple of minutes I would see her gallop past by the light of the lantern, packing another bucket of water. Eventually she managed

CHAPTER 10
MY FIRST CAR

to trip over the only non participant in our panic stricken disorder. Our big black border collie, "Li'l Pup", wanted to feel involved and was hanging about under foot which is how Mum managed to run afoul of him in the dark and empty a full bucket of cold water over him as well as inflict a considerable amount of physical discomfort when she landed on his person. He complained volubly and stumbled off into the dark to lay down beyond the danger zone. Like most dogs, he really knew how to sulk.

I soon discovered the reason it was making so much noise. I hadn't bothered to secure the throttle rod so it was turning over at a horrendous number of revs. Why would I bother to hook up the throttle ...etc.

After I cured the throttle deficiency which

lowered her enthusiasm to a clattering roar, I tightened the hose clamps making her more or less water tight. Mum sat on a nearby barrel and watched, not about to miss anything. We still were not able to speak at anything less that full screech for the racket was still very impressive and the blue flames coming out of the exhaust manifold were doing their level best to set fire to the floorboards.

The only thing left at this point in the celebration was to see if it would move under its own power.

I clambered into where the driver's seat would have been if I had owned one and delicately pressed down on one of the three pedals. She juddered momentarily, leapt ahead about three feet like a startled kangaroo and

111

stopped dead in her tracks.

Silence! She was making all the comfortable clicking noises that old engines make as they cool down. I could almost hear her say.

"That's enough for one night!"

Mumsy and I went into the house, opened the draft on the sawdust burner kitchen stove and heated up some milk for Ovaltine.

These memories are soaring back to me from nearly sixty years ago. The T is long gone, so is the house and so is old Mumsy. What I wouldn't give to return, if only for a moment or two, to those years of companionship, discovery and achievement so long ago.

CHAPTER 11
EVEN DROWNING CAN BE DIFFICULT

Consider this. Some wise man once advised any one who would listen, and few ever did, that the only place water and alcohol should be mixed is in a auto radiator, and even then, not often.

The rest of the time, in the interests of longevity, it's best to keep them as far from each other as possible.

I once worked as a deck hand on a commercial fishing boat. Our portly cook, Harry, was only passably skilled at his trade. It has been said, probably by that same wise man mentioned above, that a really good ship's cook always has at least one serious character flaw, usually nursing a vile and deadly temper. According to that dictum, Harry didn't even approach the culinary expertise that might be expected from someone of his seriously hampered social skills.

His biggest character flaw, according to my

CHAPTER 11
EVEN DROWNING CAN BE DIFFICULT

personal assessment, was that he didn't know when he'd had enough to drink.

Since booze and sea water don't mix very well, it was only a matter of time until he met with a situation where the two enemies kept company only after Harry had been foolish enough to introduce them to each other.

We were tied up along side a float. I was lying in my bunk in the foc'stle around midnight, reading, with the porthole wide open next to my left ear. The night was as quiet as a tomb except for the faint, soft creaks and popping sounds of sea life slipping into a few hours low tide hibernation until the life sustaining sea water returned.

I could hear footsteps getting louder as someone walked unsteadily along the float

CHAPTER 11
EVEN DROWNING CAN BE DIFFICULT

towards our boat. I had a hunch it was Harry but until he came closer and I could plainly hear him talking to himself, I wasn't sure.

"Lardy Jasus" he mumbled over and over, "I only get this pissed oncet a year and the way I do it,

oncet a year is enough!" Oncet a week was closer to the truth.

There was a long gap in the unsteady clumping of his gait, then a couple of quick steps, staggers, one might say, followed by a tremendous splash followed by a loud, bubbly,

"Lardy Jasus, Help, somebody save me"

Factoring in the consideration that'd be much tougher to retrieve him from the harbour dead than alive, I rushed on deck to be guided to his location by a faint stream of bubbles coming

116

up next to the float. On the verge of panic (I wasn't about to jump in and try to save him, he wasn't that good a cook) I grabbed the pike, a long aluminum pole with a fierce looking hook on one end, from the roof of the pilot house and fished around in the darkling area of the bubbles until I felt some resistance. The hook suddenly seemed to have fulfilled its purpose so I gave a great desperate heave and Harrv's head popped to the surface with the hook firmly embedded under his chin like he was actually a passing flounder I'd caught by accident. He was close enough to grasp the lifeline strung along the hull so as he gasped and bubbled, I released his chin and grabbed him by his sparse tresses.

If the hook under his chin annoyed him, it wasn't until I grabbed his hair did he really get

CHAPTER 11
EVEN DROWNING CAN BE DIFFICULT

upset. I'd forgotten how many different witch's potions from honey and sardine oil to bear fat he'd kneaded into his noggin in an effort to get more hair to grow and here was I doing my level best to rob him of what piddling success he had attained. The fact that he had been mighty close to knocking on those pearly gates and having a chinwag with Saint Peter hadn't entered his pickled mind.

By this time a crowd of interested onlookers had gathered and with their help, he was eventually dragged on board where he promptly made a concerted effort to roundhouse whoever it was he figured must have pushed him off the float.

Some months later, much the same thing happened again. I was lying in the same position

CHAPTER 11
EVEN DROWNING CAN BE DIFFICULT

when I heard his familiar staggering gait go right on past our boat and head off down the float in the wrong direction. Remembering that the only place left for him to explore in that direction was the bottom of the harbour right off the end of the float, I leapt into action.

It's amazing how a really professional drunk seems to be inflated with hydrogen and often manages to waft about at extremely slow speed like a Mickey Mouse balloon while ignoring the presence of gravity. This time I had nearly caught up to him when he weaved straight off the float into midair, slowly turned horizontal and lowered himself expertly into the harbour. I managed to get a grip on his legs before he completely disappeared. Holding his feet above water quite logically required that his other end remain where

119

air is relatively scarce. Leaving him to soak in that position for a while took much of the fight out of him.

Again, it took three able bodies to hoist fat old Cookie back onto the float and empty the bay out of him. Again, he blamed anyone and everyone close to hand and became really annoyed when we folded up with laughter since, in the kerfuffle, he'd lost half his teeth (the top half) which converted his vocal outrage into a symphony of honks and snorts and gurgling hiccups that left us far beyond feeling sympathetic. Charlie, the only worthy having been present at both christenings, carelessly got between Harry and the harbour and in a split second had been lovingly embraced by Harry as he staggered back into the drink for a second time, thus generously

120

CHAPTER 11
EVEN DROWNING CAN BE DIFFICULT

taking Charlie along for the ride. Charlie, more than a little annoyed, disencumbered himself quickly, climbed out and dripped off down the float acidly commenting that since Harry was so determined to commit suicide he could "bloody well do it without any help from me"!

Besides that, he'd just lost his favourite hat.

CHAPTER 12
OTHER WAYS TO DIG A DITCH

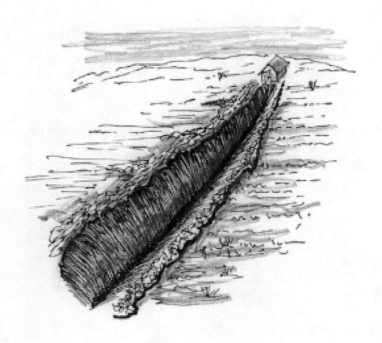

Occasionally, two completely unrelated series of events will collide like two novices on a ski hill. At

the moment of intersection, the quality and direction of both are altered forever.

CHAPTER 12
OTHER WAYS TO DIG A DITCH

Ben had been experiencing a situation in which a particular scenario replayed itself repeatedly like a stuck record player. Every morning, when Marge went to fill the kettle to make coffee, the tap would be dry. And every morning Ben would grumble off down the basement stairs, pipe wrench in hand to once again "prime" the family water pump. (This is a problem that never bedevils city dwellers whose supply of water is reliable and reasonably constant).

The process involved unscrewing a one inch pipe plug from the top of the pump and filling the cavity beneath with water from a bucketful saved the previous evening for this specific purpose. With a modicum of good luck, one application would be enough. As he replaced the plug and turned on the motor, Ben began to think

123

seriously about instituting a cure for the problem.

He had figured out what the problem was. A tiny hole was allowing air into the 200 foot suction pipe that ran from the house to the well at the bottom of the yard. Not much air got in, but it was enough to constipate the system about once every 24 hours. And it always expired at night as though it knew Ben was asleep and could be counted on not to interfere. Like most of us, Ben had been hoping that if he ignored it long enough, the problem might fix itself but these things seldom do.

His friend of many years, Andy, a powdermonkey, had been attending night school, though he loftily considered himself a mite long in the tooth to again be a student. He'd been a successful powdermonkey for most of his life, spending his days dynamiting stumps and rocks for logging roads or building sites.

It didn't matter that Andy was already considered to be an expert in the use of explosives. A new law decreed that Andy and all the other powdermonkeys must have licences to use dynamite. They were required to study various courses, then write an exam and if successful, would then be considered qualified to continue doing the very thing that, by its nature, had an uncanny knack for efficiently weeding out the unqualified.

The paperwork had come close to defeating him but he'd soldiered on because it had been made abundantly clear that, should he continue to practice his profession without a valid blaster's licence, the authorities would be pleased to provide him with room and board for a lengthy stay at the local crowbar hotel. Ergo; nightschool.

CHAPTER 12
OTHER WAYS TO DIG A DITCH

Nobody thought to delve into Andy's drinking habits before they laid a licence on him. A simple but potentially disastrous oversight.

Andy could be relied upon to get thoroughly, totally and completely blitzed once or twice a year. In the enthusiastic and single-minded manner in which he carried this out, once or twice a year was quite enough. Ben, on the other hand, got into the booze only on special occasions. The special occasion was usually accompanied by a lapse of memory. He'd forget how his last hangover carried with it all the cranial sensations of having been lobotomized with a melon scoop.

Conditions were perfect for these two avenues of life to cross and chaotically screw up the normal, reasonably modulated destinies of both men, if only for a moment in the unfolding of

CHAPTER 12
OTHER WAYS TO DIG A DITCH

their lives.

The pair hadn't seen each other for a long time. Since the office where Andy was to write the exam was in a city very close to Ben's small two acre holding, they had arranged to get together and do some "visiting".

Ben had stockpiled a few cases of Canadian beer, a deceptively mild brew which has been known to produce severe extended retching with bouts of amnesia in the uninitiated. Andy, not one to be left out, brought with him "the ingreedaments" as he called them, for a deadly drink he had valiantly fought to a draw in the Highlands of Scotland. When pressed, Andy would gleefully assemble a jug of his particular bogwater for immediate consumption.

"It don't age good", he offered, while stirring and hovering over a vat of the stuff. I have no idea how he ever discovered this timely bit of information. For reasons difficult to explain with a straight face in mixed company, the Scots had christened this mixture of Malt Whiskey, Stout and Cassis, a "Knickerdropper".

Replacing the malfunctioning suction pipe, required that Ben dig a trench, by hand, from the house to the well. As he dug and dreaded how much hard work was facing him for several weeks, Andy arrived for the visit. Andy didn't merely stroll up and say "Hi" for he was a man who truly appreciated, and had refined, the grand entrance.

Wearing a bemused and patient smile, he casually watched Ben grubbing in the ditch as though he was observing a sexton beetle burying acorpse. "Watchyadoon?" he inquired, looking down his nose.

128

CHAPTER 12
OTHER WAYS TO DIG A DITCH

Ben explained.

The two old friends were truly happy to see each other and in short order were bellied up to the bar in Ben's basement, each with a beer in hand. Quite naturally, one beer led to another. Soon it became a matter of honor that Andy be allowed to formulate a jug of his specialty.

Ben was pleasantly surprised at the innocence

this new drink exuded, though he should have been a mite suspicious when he broke into a cold sweat on his first swallow of Andy's Highland Revenge. Andy, who, when the spirit had taken him, would drink anything he could pry loose, explained very seriously to Ben that this firewater was really a special treat. Ben, in the true spirit of a polite host wishing to please his guest, put the drink to his already numbing lips and promptly

129

tumbled backwards out of his chair. The two of them were getting pretty wired while the real world rapidly receded. They'd reached the point where their mutual mumblings were interspersed with the occasional fiery exchange about nothing of any particular consequence. While working their way through a not very humble session of outrageous bragging, Ben enquired,

"How did you, mmmmph, make out with, mmmm, your blasting exam?"

Andy was obviously very proud of this achievement and taking his wallet out of his back pocket, he showed Ben his new "ticket". He could have only been happier if there had been some way to put it to use.

Sometime later they went outside to examine Ben's project. The minuscule amount of digging Ben had done seemed to arouse some faint, primeval itch in Andy who just happened to know a great deal about excavating trenches the easy way; with dynamite.

Andy squinted professionally at the vast acreage before him. Although he was already seeing two or more of everything, this virgin expanse was like waving a juicy rabbit under a badger's nose. In his mind's eye he could already see the long, even trench leading down the slope to the well. He could almost smell the burnt nitro hanging in the air. A tear almost glistened in the corner of his eye when he imagined the peaceful stillness as the last echo of the mighty explosion died away.

They weaved their way back to the basement for a few "jus' one mores."

Andy, surrendering to an overwhelming urge to blow up something, anything, decided to

131

approach Ben about the possibility of using TNT to excavate the trench but was wary of frightening him off. He made, through his alcoholic haze, what he thought was a most disarming and diplomatic suggestion.   "Lez blass the goddam thing!" he urged, a maniacal gleam in his eye. His suggestion didn't seem to come out quite as diplomatically as he'd intended.

Blasting, to Andy, was a calling, something that God had told him to do.

"Andy", God had said, "be a powdermonkey!" and Andy obeyed. Sometimes, in the dark of night, Andy would admit to himself that it might not have been God who spoke to him with such authority, but it was close enough.

At first, Ben would have no part of it for he had a phobia about explosions. The only real blast that ever caught Ben in anything less than full

132

flight was the time his neighbor's camper blew up in the driveway when the propane tank sprung a leak and some how became ignited. The trailer opened up like a giant aluminum water lily. Broke windows all over the place. Marge damply disgraced herself in the middle of the dining room carpet.

After a few more pulls of Andy's special concoction, Ben was too numb to resist anything.

Ben had a friend who had a friend who knew someone named Archie who had some dynamite stored in his barn. Ben and Andy drove over to Archie's place and moments later a few shopping bags of explosives rode home in the back of Ben's pickup. Before long, Ben was humming tunelessly to himself while happily driving a series of deep holes into the back lawn with the pointed end of a crowbar. Andy, humming

133

much the same tune, was casually stuffing the holes with sticks of powder and fuses. After a few more drinks neither of them could remember what they'd done or where they'd done it so they started all over again. When they ran out of powder, they headed back to Archie's to rearm. By then, Archie's interest had been critically piqued by the fact that Ben and Andy were obviously getting blasted in more ways than one, and, more distressingly, they were doing it without his help.

"That's a lot of bang for one hole, I think I should help", was his opening gambit.

He was delighted to be immediately invited along to the blast site. In short order the three of them were tossing back Knickerdroppers and stuffing more powder into more holes and laughing and hooting and falling all over the place.

134

CHAPTER 12
OTHER WAYS TO DIG A DITCH

It was about three in the morning when the din and foofaraw got to be too much for the neighbors and somebody called the cops. A couple of uniformed worthies arrived, tripping over Archie happily lying by himself in the dark on the front lawn, cradling a large jug of Andy's hooch. They had just started to grill him about the night's activities when Andy, whose presence was unsuspected around the other side of the house, lit a match and set the whole thing off.

It would do it no justice to merely say the night turned into day with a brilliant flash and that the hills vibrated with the roar. The bang was much more than that. Some people claimed that rocks were still coming down the next day. It was also more than Ben's already over strained constitution could stand. His life did several reruns before his bloodshot eyes as he staggered

135

CHAPTER 12
OTHER WAYS TO DIG A DITCH

off, feeling his way through the layers of drifting smoke. Covered from head to toe in dirt and now deaf as a post, he was feeling his way along, waving his arms around wildly like Merlin casting a spell when he toppled headlong into the "excavation" and passed out.

The Police, no fools they, galloped smartly off in all directions, leaving Archie and their patrol car to the whims of fate.

Andy, jerked into cold, calculating sobriety by the magnitude of the huge explosion, leapt nimbly into his truck and sped off, narrowly missing a fleeing policeman. There was no way he was going to be caught skulking about in that neighborhood.

Archie was the only real casualty. The explosion had lofted a rock about the size of a tennis shoe clear over the house, whacking him neatly between the horns and laying him out like a cold-cut.   It wasn't long before the Police returned accompanied by the Civil Defense people, three fire trucks and a half a dozen ambulances. It was quite a while before they happened to stumble across Ben. They thought he was dead until they got a whiff of him.

It took two days for the cops to come up with a sequence of events, and even then they got it all wrong. Ben and Archie were no help. They couldn't even remember their names.

The authorities concluded that, because of some obvious chunks of rusty pipe lying about that the explosion must have been caused by Methane gas lying in the pipe that had somehow been ignited. That was one mighty big "somehow" but they had to come up with something.

"Really powerful stuff, that methane", said

CHAPTER 12
OTHER WAYS TO DIG A DITCH

the police constable, stroking his chin and trying to look wise. The Fire Chief, having had some experience with arsonists and the like, was madder than Hell at being dragged out in the middle of the night merely to admire a large hole in the ground containing nothing but a cloud of acrid smoke and one unconscious drunk. He kept looking at the peacefully slumbering Ben, wondering just what he knew and if there was really any hope of ever finding out what happened. The confusing though unmistakable aroma of Malt Whiskey, Black Currants, Beer and burnt Nitro wafting about the neighborhood only added to the confusion and seemed to spell doom for any possible inquiry.

Ben had to carry water in a bucket for several days. Then he imported a Bulldozer to fill in the hole, that is, after laying new pipe in the

CHAPTER 12
OTHER WAYS TO DIG A DITCH

trench.   He was relieved   when his hearing
returned several days later. It took a carpenter
three days to rebuild the back wall of the house. In
two hours the local builder's supply had sold every
piece of glass they had.

Marge never even woke up!

CHAPTER 13
JAKE'S HALLOWE'EN BOMB

It was the proximity of Hallowe'en that had brought Jake to Peter's door that afternoon.

"I've built a bomb", whispered Jake. He held open a large brown paper bag for Peter to look into. Remembering Jake's remarkable ability to get into serious trouble without hardly trying, Peter was wary.

Once he had decided it looked harmless enough, he apprehensively inquired, "What are you going to do with it"?

I'm going to whap it with a hammer", replied Jake in a hoarse whisper, furtively peering around like a spy watching out for enemies.

"Not with me around!", replied Peter, backing away.

Jake was crestfallen. He'd expected Peter to be overjoyed at his invitation to be an active co-producer of an explosion that would carry for miles, maybe clear to the Comox glacier.

Peter would have none of Jake's screwball project without replanning the whole exercise.

"You're not going to hit that thing with a hammer, Jake, because WE are going to put a

141

fuse in it so we can be some where else when it goes off", and with that, Peter started telling Jake how they would make a fuse. Jake wasn't too sure that was a good idea. Hiding behind a tree when this wonderful bomb went off was not part of his plan.

Peter was adamant. No fuse - no Bang.

Jake surrendered.

The proper proportions of saltpetre, sulfur and charcoal from Peter's chemistry set were carefully ground together in one of Megs wooden salad bowls with a wooden stick.

The contents of the bowl were then sprinkled onto a length of wet tissue paper which they rolled up and twisted into what looked like a wet, grey shoe lace.

"What now, what now?" panted Jake,

bounding up and down.

"Now", said Peter, tucking his chin into his chest and trying to look very grave in a vain attempt to calm Jake down, "we put it away and wait 'til it's dry. Won't light unless it's dry!".

Jake, by now almost incoherent with anticipation, couldn't believe his ears.

"Wait? Wodda y'mean, wait"? Trying to hold Jake down long enough to explain the necessary and indeed, unavoidable, sequence of events was almost completely beyond Peter's capability.

"We can't do anything until the fuse is dry", Peter insisted.

"Can't we just bash it with a hammer"?, pleaded Jake.

"You'll blow your stupid head off", he

143

almost shouted, adding, "it'll be ready tomorrow. We can take it up into the park and light it off. Until then, just think about something else"!

Next morning, after breakfast, Peter sharpened a piece of wood and carefully wormed a fuse-hole into the end of Jake's bomb.

Peter carefully slid the dried fuse into the hole he'd made and to aid in this effort to produce the healthy wallop that Jake had in mind, he wound layer after layer of tape around it. When it was done, the two boys smuggled the "bomb" out of the house concealed in the paper bag.

This project must be kept a blood secret.

Several hundred yards back in the woods they pushed the bomb into a clump of deep moss on top of a old stump and Peter watched while Jake lit the fuse. In the manner of all home-made fuses, it sputtered along fitfully hissing with short periods of enthusiasm alternating with long periods of silence. A number of times, convinced that the fuse must have gone out, the boys were cautiously sneaking up to have a look when the fuse suddenly sprang back to life with a heart-stopping "whoosh" which sent the two miscreants haring back to their hideout.

The two schemers were hunkered down behind a log, waiting for the bang when Miss Hayes' Saturday Morning Riding Class posted primly into view. Miss Hayes, an elderly riding instructor, accompanied all her students each Saturday morning for an hour or two of trail riding and they were now ambling sedately along, single file towards the stump upon which rested the "Bomb".

145

CHAPTER 13
JAKE'S HALLOWE'EN BOMB

Now there isn't a horse in the world that isn't acutely psychic about danger and can smell trouble several miles away in any direction.

The lead animal, a great, addle brained gelding named Winchester, had seen the faint smoke and heard the sputtering fuse from a long way off and was all aquiver with incipient panic by the time he was abreast of the bomb. The closer he got, the more skittery he became and the tougher it became for his rider, Cynthia, to control him. She hadn't noticed the "bomb" and she had no idea what on earth was the matter with him. Winchester was snorting and gurgling with fear and twisting this way and that, not taking his bugging eyes off the stump for a split second. Cynthia was about to lose her temper and give old Winchester a good swat with her crop when the bomb went off.

Instead of the expected bang, there was a long screaming whistle and a roiling cloud of acrid white smoke. By this time, Winchester, like any horse with a strong sense of self preservation, had dumped Cynthia and lit out for somewhere else. The second horse, a brainless dimwit named Banjo, while never sure about things and being easily confused by life, was a little too slow in making decisions and had succeeded in getting only partly turned around when he and his rider were rammed full amidships and knocked flat by the fleeing Winchester.

Banjo, while dumber than Winchester, had also decided to leave. He sprang to his feet, exhaled through both nostrils with a whoosh like a broken steam pipe, and galloped at full throttle into the third horse in line, knocking them both down.

It was at this point that the "bomb" turned into a rocket and lifted off the top of the stump, and trailing a plume of dense, white smoke, arced like a guided missile above the herd and bounced off Winchester's receding rump with a loud smack.

Winchester, convinced that his worst nightmare had come true and that some sort of hideous swamp monster must have finally got it's teeth into his other end, shifted into overdrive and vaporized out of sight.

By now, things were obviously completely chaotic. Miss Hayes, at the rear of her platoon of riders, couldn't believe her senses. From the woods ahead came the sights and sounds of Custer's Last Stand. Riderless horses, coughing and snorting and wild-eyed with fear, were stumbling out of the dense smoke and stampeding off through the woods every which way. Stunned ex-riders were blindly feeling their way about in the haze while others sprinted for cover like Olympic hopefuls. Within seconds, no horses could be seen anywhere.

Nothing could ever coax old Winchester into the woods near that stump again. In fact, even the whiff of cigarette smoke or even a match being lighted was enough to fire him off like a cannon-ball, instantly, in whatever direction he happened to be pointed.

"I shoulda known better" was all Peter had to say.

CHAPTER 14
THAT $%#**? KINCADE GARDEN TRACTOR

During the second world war, when farm equipment was hard to come by, my father craftily seduced a neighbour into parting with his pet garden tractor.

150

CHAPTER 14
THAT $%#**? KINCADE GARDEN TRACTOR

It was a strange machine of bizarre design out of dubious parentage and, as events turned out, possessing of a particularly evil and foul personality. This particular design would, years later, be referred to as a "tiller" layout.

It was manufactured early in the twentieth century by the Kincade Tractor and Farm Equipment Company. Like a lot of machinery built when the industrial age was young, it carried such a grand name that everyone expected it to perform in a manner such as it's name might imply. It never came near to performing in so nobly a manner and obviously never did receive its full complement of civilized breeding.

Painted a deceptively trustworthy shade of green and high lighted in bright red, it fooled everybody. It had only one large wheel, which meant that right out of the box it was basically unstable and suffered from bunged up ear canals with some mental instability for it fell on its side at the slightest provocation.

It sported a couple of hardwood handles sticking out of the stern like a horse drawn plow. The height and angle of these handles implied that only people of titanic stature could control the direction and speed of travel of the machine by forcefully influencing these handles to port or starboard and/or by jiggling the various other controls hanging thereon. I have a mental picture of the designers at Kincade rolling about on the floor of their office shrieking with laughter, gleefully punching holes in their straw boaters. Father would have happily murdered the lot.

At first glimpse, the machine seemed to

CHAPTER 14
THAT $%#**? KINCADE GARDEN TRACTOR

have no engine and, were that true, would require someone of immense strength and will to push this four hundred pound miscreant around like a lawn mower. However, on closer inspection, it turned out the engine was hidden in the bowels of the one big wheel, those crafty chaps at Kincade company having successfully placed it where only a clairvoyant would ever find it.

As on most family farms in those days, everything worthy of consideration earned itself a name that reflected some unique facet of its personality. A lot of thinking went into the creation of something as personal as a name. Christening the Kincade became academic for after it had been unloaded from the delivery truck, it waited patiently in its upright position, pretending to be asleep until my father turned his back on it whereon it threw a fit and promptly fell on it's side, scraping down the back of his leg until it dug itself firmly into his right heel. It immediately became well endowed with several very suitable monikers, none of which us kids were ever allowed to repeat or even contemplate repeating.

Whenever father was fortunate enough to get it running, which was rarely, the first thing it did when it was working in the garden was to squeeze so much wet mud inside the one big wheel that the engine completely disappeared. Eventually it would get so enveloped in gooey sludge that it would quit running altogether whereon the operator had to be quick off the mark to dig the engine free for without immediate service, the heat from the engine would efficiently bake the mud into dark brown concrete. I'm not sure but I

154

CHAPTER 14
THAT $%#**? KINCADE GARDEN TRACTOR

suspect it was the crew at Kincade Company who invented the Jackhammer.

That machine started out in life with more design flaws than the Graff Zeppelin. The fact that the engine was buried inside the wheel was only one of its many failings. It also sported a two cycle engine which meant that getting it to run was a massive task in which the slightest deviation from the magic formulae handed down since the time of Merlin would put the engine into a dark snit from which only midnight incantations during a full moon would free it.

Japanese engineers and designers of the 1950s and later managed to get the kinks out of the two cycle engines and get them to run with a reasonable degree of civility. Before that, people would come from miles around to watch a two cycle engine that was actually running.

To get it running, Dad would insert the crank into a hole somewhere down inside the one big wheel and whirl it around, seemingly for hours before the engine would suddenly let out a series of smoky pops whereon the crank would fly out its hole and soar across the yard like a rusty boomerang. Father would stagger around in a circle, cross eyed with pain, holding his elbow or knee or crotch or whatever happened to be in the way when the crank attacked him and which he was quite sure had, in it's flight, shattered something irreplaceable. He would then call the tractor all the names that he had endowed it with the day they met.

The first thing he noticed on its maiden flight in the garden was the poor design of the cleats around the outside of the one big wheel which were meant to provide traction when plowing or the like. The design of these cleats was such that the spaces between them quickly filled in with mud and the tractor therefor became useless. His answer to this problem was to cut off the original cleats and install a set of his own design. These he fashioned out of two inch angle iron and which stuck out of the face of the wheel like steel paddles. Those little gems had no trouble gripping the soil, overalls, gloves or anything else it could reach out and snag.

This machine had other annoying habits. The engine refused to idle and the clutch had only two positions, either engaged or disengaged. There was no transitory period. The operator was either part of the scenery or watching

CHAPTER 14
THAT $%#**? KINCADE GARDEN TRACTOR

it flash past.

The operator, in this case, my Dad, was forced to take one hand off the right handle to engage the clutch. The abruptness with which the clutch connected the engine to the wheel meant that he usually hadn't time to reconnect with the handle before the machine was fading off in the distance, spraying topsoil in all directions with complete abandon followed by Father in hot pursuit, again, addressing it by name.

Few people other than professional sprinters could stay with that tractor since the engine wouldn't slow down. Like a bicycle, it would stay vertical as long as it was haring along at a full gallop. Dad once said he felt kind of superfluous, flapping along in the slipstream like a burgoo.

The last time I ever saw him use it was, in

every dimension, a disaster. He had discovered that he could keep both hands on the controls if he banged the clutch lever into place with his forehead.

On that last memorable day, this is just what he did and away they went. The one big wheel, spinning like a ditch digger and hurling great clods of earth into the air, was desperately trying to get away from my father. Dad, his leading edges slathered in muddy lumps, couldn't see where they were heading.

They bounced across the garden through row after row of the nicely spaced seedlings it was supposed to be cultivating. When it came to the end of the garden it was going at much too great a clip to change direction. It hurried over a sort of berm or levee at the edge of a deep ditch and,

159

without missing a beat, towed my father into the water.

He wasn't about to give up at this stage. The tractor, roaring throaty defiance and issuing great clouds of smoke and steam managed to get its new, highly efficient traction lugs into the page wire fence on the far side of the ditch and rapidly climbed up about six feet, lug over lug, with Dad on its back like a bronco buster at the local rodeo.

Dad hung on. He would never admit defeat. This battle had become personal. With a strangled roar, he dragged it off the fence and he and the tractor disappeared out of sight into the ditch while he wrestled it as he would have an alligator, to a standstill and finally, silence. Silence, that is, except for his outraged roaring skillfully blessing the thing at the top of his lungs.

He reappeared moments later, festooned with all the greenery and mud one usually associates with ditches and swampwater and, his rage giving him the strength of six men, carried the recalcitrant tractor in his arms like an unconscious prisoner, finally dumping it on the ground. He then stumped off, mumbling to himself, to get a rope. Between all of us, we dragged it up the hill to his shop, numb with fear that one of us was going to break into insane giggling. That would have really corked it!

When it found it couldn't escape, I think the poor thing died of a broken heart or whatever it had down inside that one big wheel. It never ran again.

CHAPTER 15
WASPS ARE SUPER MOTIVATORS

It was one of those warm, lazy days of early summer that can arrive anytime from early May through into late June. The trees had pretty well finished with their early blooming and the air was brimming with the sounds of millions of different kinds of bugs, all hurrying to get their duties finished well before the cool days of autumn arrived.

Even when life is bursting forth in every direction, there's a peaceful richness to behold for those who'll listen. It's there, oh, so briefly, at this particular time of year.

This is also the time of year specifically designed for young boys. School, at last, is out and hordes of them, no longer suffering the itching confines of the school room, trundle about the countryside like troops of bandits in search of adventure. There's always a nondescript dog or two lolloping around the fringes of the group, also on the lookout for something exciting. Maybe today there'll be an adventure that requires some digging; maybe to get blissfully lucky and flush a

CHAPTER 15
WASPS ARE SUPER MOTIVATORS

rabbit or a cat.

In a tall Arbutus tree that stood beside the trail to the garden hung a huge wasp's nest. It was about forty feet up, its grey mass nearly invisible, well hidden in the mottled shadows cast by the leathery green leaves. Somewhat larger than a well inflated football, it was home base for several thousand industrious and consistently truculent yellowjackets. On the scale of bellicosity, they lie midway between a Honeybee, which is generally mild and inoffensive and a Hornet, the wasp's larger black and white striped cousin who mainlines steroids and whose dedicated hostility is unsurpassed while its sting is on a par with a direct hit from an anti tank rifle.

They had constructed their home well, these wasps, incorporating several of the bright red

164

branches into the structure, making them an integral part of the whole. Their architect had planned carefully and they undoubtedly felt quite secure in their grey paper sack.

No invasion plans were more carefully organized during WWII. The battle being hatched by the eager, freckled faced marauders standing below it on the ground was not without flaws. The biggest problem was the height of the quarry. It was hard to get off a good, clean shot from directly below with a rock big enough to do any real damage. Standing directly below was hazardous because angle of incidence is reduced should the wasps counter attack and a rapid retreat become necessary. No matter how fast you pick up those feet and put 'em down, there's no way you can outrun an infuriated wasp whose descending angle of attack can literally cut you off at the pass. And there was more than just a smattering of the barbarous blighters up there. Secondly, there was also some vague law of physics to consider; something about a rock, having been thrown straight up contained a clear proclivity to come straight down again, probably zonking one of the invading force on his dome.

We threw quite a number of rocks at the nest before someone managed a telling blow which gave it a pretty good shaking up and a couple of the little buzzers came down to check us out. Devout cowards that we were, we all galloped off in a herd to hide around behind the Barn, giddy with excitement. As soon as things quietened down, we gathered up more ammunition and returned to lay down a second barrage.

Holy Cow, did they ever find us rapidly the second time. Mike was just winding up to throw when, Bam, right between the eyes. Like a herd of panicky Gnus, we charged off in complete disorder. These Wasps were small but they sure caught on quicker than we'd expected. We hung around in the dark tool shed, waiting for things to cool down and laughing at Mike's face which was swelling up like the Goodyear blimp. He wasn't laughing quite as hard as the rest of us. We had to wait quite a stretch before launching the third attack.

It was this frantic third assault that finally rattled the nest loose from the branches and allowed it to tumble, spewing wasps, to the ground. A good thing too, for they would have

167

figured out our modus operandi had we found it necessary to launch a fourth attack. We had already considered this as a distinct hazard hardly worth the effort.

As the nest came down, we all lit out again. Mike, who by now was almost unrecognizable, beat the fastest retreat of all. He easily out paced the rest of us to the tool shed.

Paddy, my Border Collie, was very personable dog. She would "point" crows when she and I went hunting. She could out run a cat, in front or behind. But most of all she loved to retrieve things, a point I had stupidly forgotten.

I guess you've already figured it out. Paddy arrived at the barn within seconds proudly carrying the nest into the tool shed and expecting to be praised and petted for her ability.

168

CHAPTER 15
WASPS ARE SUPER MOTIVATORS

Together, we had been wondering just what we were going to do next when that question was instantly resolved.

We did nothing more as a group. Now, it was every man for himself. And Paddy followed each of us in turn, trying to lay the nest and its now totally delirious occupants at our feet. She just couldn't find a pair of feet that stayed in one place long enough for her to carry out her desire. Having had a few seconds premonition of what she had in mind, I was already under way and picking up speed. Mike, second in line, tripped and fell precisely in the doorway of the shed, failing miserably in his ambition not to get stung again. Failed several times, actually.

I made it to the dairy, zipped inside and locked the door behind me. Through the window I could

169

CHAPTER 15
WASPS ARE SUPER MOTIVATORS

see the sequence of events on the other side of the glass. Mike was still making much better time than any one else but clearly hadn't thought out his avenue of escape. He was ricocheting about the barn yard looking for a hiding place and was on the verge of outrunning them when several got into his hair. Ahead lay the horse trough full of water. That was all he needed. With a tremendous splash he disappeared from my field of view.

Charles, on the other hand, decided to head straight home, since he didn't know his way around our place well enough to locate a safe hideout. The last I saw of him, he was running down the driveway flat out, followed by black and white dog carrying something grey, followed by a dark cloud of something. The way he was flapping his arms, he was on the verge of become airborne.

CHAPTER 15
WASPS ARE SUPER MOTIVATORS

It was at this juncture in my dissolute youth that I experienced what people mean when they said their blood froze, for, out of the corner of my eye, I spotted my Father shuffling slowly up the trail from the garden, headed directly into the war zone. Now the only thing I feared more than an angry wasp was an infuriated father, and even though there were thousands of wasps as far as the eye could see, I'd still rather face the wasps. I stayed put where I was in my safe house and waited for the end of the world. As Dad got closer to the Arbutus tree, he started to bob and weave like a shadow boxer, waving his arms about and slapping himself enthusiastically. He didn't walk any faster or appear to become enraged or indulge in any of a dozen reactions I would have expected of him. He just kept plodding straight ahead, occasionally hopping straight up like he was

CHAPTER 15
WASPS ARE SUPER MOTIVATORS

hurdling an imaginary saw horse. And he kept up a steady slapping and batting at the air. I could not imagine what he thought was happening.

Sometime later, while I cowered in a corner of the kitchen in fear that I might be "found out" and catch the blame for his discomfort, I heard him mention to Mother, quite casually, I thought, that a Bee had taken a dislike to him as he walked up from the garden.

"I thought I was going to be stung," he said with genuine hurt in his voice.

A BEE? I could plainly see the dense cloud of wasps from my vantage point a few hundred feet away. And I found it astonishing that he hadn't been stung even once. I had watched him flailing his arms about like an outraged politician speaking in semaphore. And he didn't get stung. The Gods had

172

CHAPTER 15
WASPS ARE SUPER MOTIVATORS

indeed been kind to me.

Ever after that day, Charles became decidedly rattled whenever he so much as heard a flying insect of any kind. Mike eventually shrunk back to normal and the only serious casualty was poor Paddy. She was decidedly under the weather for a few day but soon bounced back and forever displayed an intense hatred for anything that buzzed and flew about.

I can well do without them too, thank you very much.

CHAPTER 16
DUCK! DUCK! HERE COMES CHUCK

When I was just a tad we had a young fellow named Chuck boarding with our family while he attended school. His normal home was so far out in the backwoods that they hadn't even

CHAPTER 16
DUCK! DUCK! HERE COMES CHUCK

started to grow the trees they might someday build a school out of.

He was an eager, idiotic, freckle faced optimist who greeted each day as though it had been invented just for him. His demeanor was such that whenever you spoke to him, he hung on every word and exuded all the characteristics of someone who completely understood everything you were saying. He might as well have been asleep.

He would maintain clear eye contact, nod sagely at just the right moment and even interject words or short phrases indicating how thorough was his understanding. It wouldn't be until sometime later, after the four horsemen had come and gone, that the true depth of his understanding, or complete lack of it, became

CHAPTER 16
DUCK! DUCK! HERE COMES CHUCK

clear.

This was something that my father could never fathom. He was a very logical person and would go to great lengths to make sure he had explained the nuances in any given situation clearly and succinctly to everyone even remotely connected with the project.

Sometime later, when the supposedly innocuous situation had taken on all the aspects of a race riot, he would discover that, through some sort of hypnotic miscue, he must have actually said nothing at all. He got to thinking that maybe he'd dreamed the whole thing up.

Upon recall, it seems to me he spent a lot of time looking very stunned and confused.

"Didn't I say ...." he would query, leaving out the part that he thought he'd said Because

CHAPTER 16
DUCK! DUCK! HERE COMES CHUCK

he didn't finish his question, we couldn't answer it. We were, however, willing to ad lib.

"Noooo", we'd chorus, looking at each other blankly.

He would stand with his head leaned to one side with his mouth slightly open and peer with doubting eye at his collected antagonists.

So it was in this context that my father decided to relocate our flock of Peking ducks, During the course of the move it was decided to dig a new pond adjacent to the main water line so that a pipe could be led from the main line, a tap installed and thereby be a means to supply the ducks with that which they love above all else. Lots and lots of water.

Chuck was volunteered (spell appointed) to the task of digging the pond. My old dad

CHAPTER 16
DUCK! DUCK! HERE COMES CHUCK

accompanied him to the construction site and explained the process very carefully. Dad walked back and forth pointing out where lay the main water line, scratching lines on the ground with a sharp stick and putting pegs at the corners and going over the reasons why not to dig anywhere else. Chuck nodded. Dad then explained again the wheres and whyfors of the location of the pond, going into great detail. Again Chuck nodded knowingly. I think I remember him completely disarming my dad by saying,

"I understand!"

I knew he didn't understand. He never understood anything. He didn't understand why it wouldn't be wise to ride his bike on the four inch wide hand railing across the bridge spanning the fifty foot deep canyon. During his free fall to the

CHAPTER 16
DUCK! DUCK! HERE COMES CHUCK

creek below I think he came about as close to understanding anything as he ever did.

About an hour after my Dad left him to his own devices, Chuck was industriously excavating the new pond, when my mother suddenly turned from the sink to say to my father,

"That's funny, there's no water pressure"!

My father leapt to his feet, shouted "Goddam" and shot out the door, tripping over the dog in the process. The dog, yanked out a sound sleep to find he was being used as a stepladder by a raving lunatic, started to take a round out of my dad who simply didn't have the time or inclination to hang about to accept the challenge.

The source of the problem became obvious to dad while he was still several hundred feet

CHAPTER 16
DUCK! DUCK! HERE COMES CHUCK

from the construction project. A fountain of water was shooting about fifty feet into the air. It looked like we had acquired our very own private geyser. Its spouting would stop every few seconds as Chuck tried valiantly to stem the flow with various parts of his anatomy whereon he would have to pick himself up out of the mud from several feet away, rush back and try again.

He was quite a sight

It took the rest of the day to shut down the system and repair the pipe with quick setting cement.

Chuck later explained his actions.

"I was digging along when I found a large black root all covered in tar and thick wire. I didn't know what it was so I gave it a big whack with the pick and all the water came out.

CHAPTER 16
DUCK! DUCK! HERE COMES CHUCK

He actually looked proud of himself

I could tell from the dark look in Dad's eye that he required revenge in order to ever rest well again in this lifetime. Since Chuck was approximately the same age and size as the rest of us, he earned the same punishment.

He didn't understand that, either, but it did compensated my Father somewhat for the soul satisfying murder he had been cheated out of.

CHAPTER 17
PUNKY WAS A WATCH DOG
(THAT EVERYBODY NEEDED TO WATCH)

Punky was a Dachshund. Old, quiet and arthritic. He harboured a pathological need to chew on things. Things like ankles and legs, for instance. And he seemed to think he had been appointed by St. Fido himself to be a watchdog. At least, that is how he conducted himself.

The thing was that Punky was very slow. He didn't seem to be "all there", y'know, sort of like a spoonful short of a bowl. But I'm even not too sure about that, for given a choice, he'd always bite the Anglican Minister first which says a great deal in his favour.

He didn't have the frenetic drive of your average watchdog. Long after the danger had arrived and had almost settled in, he could be spotted trudging single mindedly into view like he was a clockwork dog running on daylight saving time. With a distant look in his eye, as though he was fulfilling some cosmic need to attend to other

183

things while acting as though keeping watch was truly the farthest thing from his mind.

While the supposed miscreant who had caught Punky's attention was standing still and had been doing so for some time, maybe drawing Punky's owner into a conversation, Punky would meander up and just as the victim was saying, "Oh isn't he a cute little number", Punky would bite 'em. Not quickly or with any vehemence. No barking or threatening roars. Just a slow, disarming opening of the mouth, then a deliberate head rotation followed by a slow forward lean to enable him to get a real hold then an even slower closing of the jaws. The victim all the while hadn't the slightest idea that an attack was in progress until the incredible pain indicated

CHAPTER 17
PUNKY WAS A WATCH DOG
(THAT EVERYBODY NEEDED TO WATCH)

that his foot was slowly being amputated and that some sort of immediate intervention was acutely necessary.

Punky's owner, an elderly lady of impeccable heritage in the finest Victorian manner, tried her best to keep an eye on Punky for it had been highly embarrassing more than a few times as several bystanders tried valiantly to separate the biter and the bitee. Punky seldom enjoyed the opportunity to really get his teeth locked onto something worthwhile and when he did, he wasn't about to give up his hold without a fight. More than once the aggrieved person ended up lying on the lawn with Punky also lying on the lawn, still firmly grafted and apparently asleep while several people discussed how to get the dog to let go. My approach would have been to remove the dogs lower jaw but not everyone, particularly the owner, saw it my way.

A startling number of different methods were tried over the years to separate Punky and his victims. Nothing worked. Someone suggested feeding some Propane gas up his snoot and then lighting him off like a bomb but Punky's owner wouldn't hear of it. I suppose she, quite correctly I think, surmised that Punky would be distributed fairly generously around the local shrubbery and it would be very difficult to gather up enough to bury. And there was no guarantee that the victim still would be rid of the one thing he wanted to lose; Punky's teeth. One itinerant salesman clobbered him pretty good with a copy

186

of Encyclopedia Britannica but Punky's German heritage saw only the insult contained therein so he closed his eyes and dug in even deeper for the long term.

The only successful alternative to the problem was reluctantly discovered one afternoon when a young lady of the Hippie persuasion walked up the driveway and was surprised to find that she had suddenly sprouted this silent but persistent growth on her leg. Instead of leaping about and acting the aggrieved idiot, she gently kneeled down and started caressing Punky and telling him in a soft understanding voice what a fine dog he was and how she could easily see he was just doing his job as he saw fit. He growled for a minute or two, then he suddenly relaxed his

187

grip, slowly turned about, looked up her with rheumy eyes and trundled off across the lawn. His enemy had become his friend and having capitulated, didn't need further intimidation nor extended dedicated gnawing.

I think it was Abraham Lincoln who said, "The way to get rid of an enemy is to make him into a friend".

This was one time when "Love your enemy" really came to pay off.

CHAPTER 18
THOSE JEEZLY MICE

When I was about ten, a rather large, gregarious chap at school attempted to stuff my head through a basket ball hoop in the school gym. As a result of this friendly gesture, my nose

CHAPTER 18
THOSE JEEZLY MICE

was sacrificed and my sniffer lost virtually all of
its natural talent. Even today, I can catch no more
than an occasional whiff, and even then nearly
always of something that has been dead and
lying about in the sun for several weeks.

Quite a few years later; married; children;
rented house; mouse invasion. One day my wife
"de jour", said, "Will you check out that cupboard
by the stove. It smells awfully like something died
in there." I counted heads; kids, (2), dogs, (1)
cats, (2) and, as no-one was missing and since I
couldn't smell anything untoward I assumed it
was something she had imagined and forgot the
whole thing. A few days later, the odor had
become thick enough to shovel, even to my
benumbed sensibilities, which meant that people

were crossing the street as they went by our house. I decided to investigate.

What I found was a virtual storm of small furry creatures with bright, beady eyes and big pink ears who ricocheted about the cupboard at close to the speed of sound. I found where they had mined an entrance at the bottom corner so I plugged that and with no further ado, planned an attack.

I took several arm loads of books from the bookcase and built the great wall of Mousedom all around the cupboard entrance so if any came out, they couldn't get away. I didn't want to have to do this twice. Then I emptied everything from the cupboard, checking each item for stowaways. When the cupboard was bare, it was truly bare.

CHAPTER 18
THOSE JEEZLY MICE

There wasn't a mouse in sight. I checked again. There was no way for them to get out so they had to be in there somewhere. I had by now pretty well squeezed right inside, looking for them when suddenly, one popped up from behind a shelf, raced across the back of my hand, tried to get up my sleeve and then disappeared behind another shelf. Within a fraction of a second I had whacked my head on the door frame and sprained several fingers getting out of the cupboard and was half a block away, picking up speed. Jeez, I hate those furry little rockets.

Fortunately (I don't know why) the door of the cupboard had a small window where, with a flashlight, I could stand outside and still see what they were up to. When they found their hiding

CHAPTER 18
THOSE JEEZLY MICE

places all gone and their escape route blocked, they became quite agitated and went bucketing around the inside with such gusto it was like observing an automatic washing machine full of mice on the spin cycle.

I could see it was time to make those two pussy cats earn some of their keep. I opened the cupboard door, closed them both inside and peered through the window to watch as they did their foul work. Foul work? Not a chance! They were merely confused, looking about in bewilderment. Then one of the mice did the "jump up and run somewhere else" routine and both cats nearly died of fright. In an instant they were both standing on tip toes pretending it was Halloween, their fur standing straight out like a couple of multi hued bottle brushes. When the mouse disappeared, they both put on the best "I'll slaughter 'em" act I've ever seen. They crouched, their tails twitching, working their feet around as though getting ready to launch an attack when one of the mice replayed the jump up and run somewhere else routine. Both cats became immediately hysterical. The routine palled when they both had nervous breakdowns and merely looked the other way. One even thoughtfully raised it's paw out of the way as the mice went tearing past them.

I opened the door and watched as the panic stricken cats disappeared at high speed into the night. They didn't need a second invitation.

CHAPTER 18
THOSE JEEZLY MICE

The only reserve for murder and mayhem I now held was Mr. Wiggins, our Old English Sheep dog. He'd moved in closer and was now lying within the "great wall", watching the fun. Mr. Wiggins was a true softie. He loved a good scrap and expertly made all the roaring, murderous snarling noises that punctuate a healthy dog fight, but, to my knowledge, never even laid a tooth on an opponent. I guess he never caught on to all the nuances involved for he often arrived home after an armed foray looking like he'd been run over by a lawn aerator.

I put on a very tough pair of leather gloves and returned to the cupboard. Grabbing one of the mice by the tail as it roared by at high speed, I flipped it onto the floor next to Mr. Wiggins who

195

CHAPTER 18
THOSE JEEZLY MICE

calmly watched it slip beneath him to hide in all that dense fur. I exhorted him wildly with "Get it, Wiggins" and "Kill it, Wiggins", waving my arms like I was sending semaphore. He continued to look at me with those great big brown eyes, wordlessly asking for further directions. He finally stood up and the mouse dropped out of his fur like a survivor of the Hindenburg and scuttled across the floor. Further enthusiastic exhortations on my part finally goaded him into action. He gently leaned forward and scooped up the mouse with an apologetic slurp then sat down, his cheeks puffed out, peering at me, awaiting further instructions. I kept up my noisy urging when, not understanding what was expected of him, he slowly leaned forward, put his chin on the floor

CHAPTER 18
THOSE JEEZLY MICE

and opened his mouth whereon the mouse, drenched in slobber, stepped daintily to the floor like the Queen disembarking from royal barge, staggered off, stopping to raise and shake each leg in turn.

That did it for me. No more Mr Niceguy! I finally got to put my huge 1898 copy of Debrett's Peerage to good use. I wrapped it in a plastic bag and skillfully flattened each rodent as it hove into view. Britain's House of Lords was finally put to good use.

CHAPTER 19
MY NEW YEAR'S RESOLUTION
(PARKED)

A number of years ago, on New Year's Eve, I was driving along one of the many back roads near my home considering if there was any one particular thing I could swear off, or on, at twelve midnight. I finally decided that I would, as often as possible, do something every day to help my fellow man.

Once that exhaustive little mental game had been settled, I was forced to put it into action when I came across Harold, a casual acquaintance, waving at me while standing alongside the road as though waiting for a bus. I pulled over, parked and walked back to offer any assistance, feeling more than a little smug that the opportunity has arisen so quickly to possibly help my fellow man.

From his agitated state, it was obvious he was in some kind of a bind. He would stare down the fifty foot embankment beside the road for a few seconds as if expecting a Sasquatch to appear, then look left and right along the road as if wishing someone or something would hurry into view.

We howdied and it was then I noticed Harold's Model T Roadster Pick-up reposing up side down between some trees on the flat bushy area at the bottom of the bank.

Harold's Model T sputtered out of the Henry's factory around 1920. It was called a "Roadster Pick Up" or a "Gentleman Farmer's Sporty Runabout", which meant it had a single bench seat for the driver and a reasonably small passenger, a flimsy canvas convertible top and a small freight box that hung like an afterthought on the stern, like a bustle. The T was about as high as it was long which gave it a spooky ability to suddenly, without warning, turn turtle - which had a lot to do with why Harold had parked the car it where presently lay.

"Did you park it down there on purpose?" I asked, chortling at my own audacious wit.

"No," he grumped in a hurt voice, "I was crowded off the road , just lucky I wasn't killed".

"Have you come up with a set of plans about how to get her out of there"? I queried.

"No", he answered, stammering slightly and looking down at his Model T with an intensely worried look.

"I sent a message to my brother to come and give me a some help", he said, peering hopefully into the distance.

"Well, I'll give you a hand until he gets here. Maybe the two of us can roll her over back onto her wheels".

Boy oh boy, was I in for a surprise!

201

CHAPTER 19
MY NEW YEAR'S RESOLUTION

All the time we'd been standing around, shooting the breeze, every so often I would hear a sound like a distant cattle auctioneer but it wasn't loud enough to really pique my attention. It was also too irregular to command exploration.

"How's your wife?" I enquired, making conversation.

"I dunno", he said, glancing worriedly at the upturned T again, "she's still underneath". He turned and pointed his thumb over his shoulder...and added,

"I'll bet she's pretty mad!"

The T was sitting foursquare like a large upturned washtub with a wheel at each corner and an acutely irate Minnie trapped beneath it. I didn't think his lack of serious concern was at all chivalrous until I remembered that Minnie was at

CHAPTER 19
MY NEW YEAR'S RESOLUTION

least twice his size and sported a vile temper that she had been cultivating since birth.

Suddenly I figured it out. He didn't want Minnie getting out from under that car until he was quite sure she would not have the opportunity to beat the daylights out of him. In lieu of that, all he wanted a really healthy head start. That explained the nervous glances toward the scene of the upset.

I practically forced him to come down to his car with me and together we started to roll it up on it's side. Boy, he was as nervous as a bomb disarmer when the ticking stops. As soon as we'd lifted the car sufficiently to give Minnie enough clearance and it began to look like she was about to escape, he'd drop his half and run up the bank like crazy. I couldn't hold it up by myself so it would drop with a thump and the hooting from underneath would intensify even more. When we finally got it high enough for long enough, she came roaring out from under like an Angel of Death and it was a good thing for Harold that he was pretty agile. From the amount of screeching she was doing, I couldn't blame him for clearing out. He dodged back and forth around me, and the car, always keeping himself on the opposite side from Minnie. As soon as he spotted an opening, he galloped up the bank like a bear going up a tree.

Minnie was cradling one arm with the other. I'm no doctor but I could see from the angle of dangle of that held arm that it was well and truly broken. She started homing in on me like the whole thing was my fault so I adroitly joined

204

CHAPTER 19
MY NEW YEAR'S RESOLUTION

Harold at the top of the bank where we roosted like a couple of crows on a fence, eyeing the situation. We sat by the side of the road up where it was safe and watched Minnie ripping and tearing down below while we discussed our plan of action, or lack of it. Her ranting and raving from the woods below us finally grew fainter. She was either running out of air, or blood, or both. Finally she grew quiet.

"I'm pretty sure she's got a broken arm" I offered.

"Good" said Harold.

I didn't know whether he meant "good" that she wasn't very seriously injured or "good" because now she wouldn't be able to get a good swat at him, at least until she had a cast on her arm and had hopefully cooled down. I suspect

205

Harold never looked very far into the future. If Min had ever nailed him with the cast she eventually wore, she'd a likely killed him.

I promised Minnie that I'd take her to the hospital for repairs if she'd behave herself. She said she would, and she did. I helped her up the bank while Harold shouted encouragement from a half a block away. He was happy to stay with the car while I delivered Minnie to the hospital. That way it was safer all around.

After that, whenever I saw Harold on the side of the road, I just gave him a cheerful wave and stepped on the accelerator. So much for that New Years Resolution.

CHAPTER 20
JES' TRY TO MAKE UP YOUR MIND, DEAR.

It was shortly after my ninth birthday that I began to sense that there was something really odd about my Father.

CHAPTER 20
JES' TRY TO MAKE UP YOUR MIND, DEAR.

He knew just about all anybody needed to know about horses. He was associated with the cavalry during the Boer war and did much the same job during the first World War. He had a whole encyclopedia of horsey information stored in his head. He always knew what to do to keep our own horses healthy and generally cooperative. However, that was the point where his expertise ended in regards to transportation. He could build steam engines and all the accouterments that went with them but prop him up in front of a gasoline engine and it was game over. I always assumed it was the fumes from the gasoline addled his brain.

He was about seventy when he finally gave up trying to figure out how to understand the automobile and how to get it to do what he

CHAPTER 20
JES' TRY TO MAKE UP YOUR MIND, DEAR.

wanted. The end to his driving career arrived one Summer morning in a most innocuous manner. It was almost as though he had been expecting the car to act up and would accept this to be the final wedge that came between him and the automobile.

Father was a very natty dresser. Pearl grey suit with waistcoat; dress boots, not shoes, polished like chrome; immaculate white shirt, conservative tie, matching grey homburg sitting squarely on his head and occasionally, a silver tipped cane. He was a picture of breeding and wealth. The breeding showed. The wealth was something else again.

With my father driving, my mother sitting beside him and me in the back seat, we started off in the 1926 Willy's Whippet to do some business in the local town, about ten miles away. We weren't yet a mile from home before the trouble started. Dad, who could always feel the mood of a team of horses by the messages that traveled up the reins to his hands, was totally unprepared for what happened with the Whippet. The steering wheel told him nothing. He could tell if one of the horses was tired or feeling under the weather; if there was an unseen danger up ahead and a whole host of other hints about the environment. With a car, even having reins wouldn't have told him much, especially since he didn't know the language.

While driving, he kept up an earnest, necessarily one sided conversation with the car. When it became necessary to stop, he'd press on the brake pedal alright, but at the same time he's

210

CHAPTER 20
JES' TRY TO MAKE UP YOUR MIND, DEAR.

talk to the car like it was a horse or a team of horses. "Ease up, Girls", he'd say and if the car failed to slow as quickly as he wished, he'd pull back on the steering wheel and start to swear at it, blessing it roundly in terminology never heard in Sunday School. I thought it strange that he could be so talented about so many other things without having the slightest notion of what made a car go.

On this day, the trouble started as we approached a fork in the road. My Mother, who acted as navigator said, "Fred, we'll need to go down Berridge Street to deliver the milk to so and so". Dad started to slow down to make the curve, all the while saying things like, "Alright, easy now" and so on and was partly around the corner when Mother said, "Oh forget it, We'll deliver it on the way home". Dad turned the car back on to it's

211

original course but the no- mans land between the two roads was now perilously close when Mother said, "Oh, Goodness, I forgot, I promised we'd deliver it on the way in to town"

Dad bravely started to herd the Whippet again onto the side road but it was too late. With a great roar of cusswords, he split the difference and pulled back on the steering wheel so enthusiastically he almost ended up in the back seat with me. By the time he got stopped, he'd dropped the front wheels off the road and over the bank.

After ten minutes of engine roaring and rocking of wheels, we were still stuck. There was a rich, hot oily smell emanating from underneath somewhere and the rear wheels were slowly digging themselves into their own ruts.

CHAPTER 20
JES' TRY TO MAKE UP YOUR MIND, DEAR.

Dad suddenly got out and ordered Mother to get into the driver's seat. Considering that Mother had driven a car only twice before in her life and they were Model Ts that don't even have a gear shift, even I could see that there was disaster afoot.

"I'm going to push on the front bumper", he said. "when I say so, step on the gas a bit and let the clutch out". So saying, he went around to the front and put his shoulder up against the radiator somewhere, grunted loudly which Mother took to be about following the instructions regarding stepping on the gas and so on which she did. The Whippet never hesitated. It enthusiastically leapt back onto the road. Mother had backed it out so skillfully that dear old Dad was left lying face down in the mud

213

CHAPTER 20
JES' TRY TO MAKE UP YOUR MIND, DEAR.

"Oh Dear", said Mother, remembering Dad's short fuse.

"Oops", said I, ducking down out of sight. This was no time to be a smart ass.

She moved the car out of the middle of the intersection while Dad, looking more like a compost heap than anything else, silently climbed into the passenger's seat, squared up his hat, looked solemnly straight ahead through the windshield and instructed Mother to "drive on".

That was the last time Dad ever drove a car. Not only that, it was the last time he even rode in that particular car. They never had seen eye to eye. It truly was a stand off.

From then on, Mother was the chauffeur and Dad stayed home.

214

CHAPTER 21
JUST FISHIN' FOR THE HALIBUT

Coop was a crafty old fisherman, skilled and stubborn. A skinny, raunchy, impatient bachelor with a sharp, crooked beak of a nose

215

and wrinkly brown, outdoor skin who lived only to fish. A lifetime of trolling around Cape Mudge had taught him to think like a fish and when on the water, he was seldom taken unawares. But this day was to be different. Late afternoon, close to shore, trolling in shallow water, Coop thought he'd hooked bottom. Grumbling, he watched the rod arc back under tension and, rather than take a chance on breaking his line and losing his gear, he notched the old Fairbanks Morse into reverse and kachuffed slowly backwards towards the hang-up, reeling in his slacking line as he backed.

Moments later, when he looked over the side to analyze the situation, his scalp prickled and he immediately thought of several other places he'd rather be.

216

CHAPTER 21
JUST FISHIN' FOR THE HALIBUT

He swore bitterly under his breath for a few moments for lying quietly at the end of his line, thoughtfully planning its next campaign, was the biggest halibut he'd ever seen. It was longer than Coop was high and outweighed him at least two to one.

Although rare, halibut weighing over eight hundred pounds have been landed. One hundred to four hundred pounds is not uncommon.

They are a simply and efficiently designed flatfish, with a mouth, gills and a pair of eyes hung on one side of the leading edge and a huge flat tail at the other. Between these is one, enormous stupid muscle keeping the two ends apart, or together, depending on your point of view. Nearly as wide as they are long, they eat almost anything made of meat left lying around,

217

on or near the bottom.

Coop's experience with halibut had left him wary as a barn cat in a dog pound. He once hooked a much smaller model, managing to haul it aboard where it promptly tried to flap the boat into kindling. Coop, hopping around like a duck stamping out a grass fire, was trying not to get his legs broken He came close to scuttling his boat by accidentally chopping a hole in the bottom while flailing away with a hatchet, trying to decapitate the hovering fish. After receiving a couple of healthy thumps on the noggin, the halibut must have felt hurt and rejected for it expertly flopped over the side and disappeared, taking along Coop's fishing tackle.

Now, as he watched, his unwelcome quarry started to move, slowly at first, ominously, silently, surging towards deeper water.

Coop was too much the fighter to give up easily. He released the drag brake on his reel, engaged the clutch on the engine and ran the boat a few yards to beach it solidly onto the gravel where he shut off the engine. He would have preferred to battle this monster while standing on solid ground but it had become obvious he wasn't going to have time to get out of the boat and onto the beach. His adversary was now on its way to distant parts under a full head of steam, the reel screaming as the line ran out. Coop had only seconds left to do something, anything, before his adversary callously stole all his gear again. He kept up a steady stream of invective, alternating between quiet, stiff jawed epithets and all out expert cursing.

219

CHAPTER 21
JUST FISHIN' FOR THE HALIBUT

Coop knew this huge fish could easily generate many times the amount of tension the line could tolerate and he drew on all his years of fishing skill to delicately keep just enough drag on the line to exhaust the monster without permitting it to break free.

It would have been easier to exhaust a nuclear submarine.

The battle raged for two hours. It was nearly dusk when Coop lost his footing on the floorboards of his boat. The fish gave an extra enthusiastic lunge and Coop flipped end over end, landing "arse up" as he later described it, in water nearly to his waist.

That was when he lost the first family heirloom; his favorite Harris Tweed cap.

Out of the corner of his eye he could see it

drifting resolutely away in a westerly direction but he was much too busy to go after it.

He still had hopes of eventually winning this fight but they faded considerably when he unwittingly stepped into a hole in the muddy bottom and, sputtering and bubbling, disappeared from sight. When he surfaced and finished spluttering, his favorite store-bought teeth with his favorite pipe still clenched firmly between them had disappeared. It was probably all that coughing. He released the reel brake and made a lunge for the shore. It was too late. There was no more line on the reel.

Coop figured, in retrospect, that this must have also been about the time when his favorite spectacles fell off his face. He hadn't noticed them missing at the time, what with all that salt water and stuff in his eyes. His adversary had clearly gained the upper hand, or flipper. Coop could no longer retain his footing on the slippery bottom and was slowly, surely, being maneuvered into deeper and deeper water. First he lost one shoe in the muddy bottom, then the other.

With no choices left, he was beyond the point of no return. He no longer had the solid footing needed to snap the line so he sadly relaxed his tired grip on the rod and fuzzily watched its inexorable progress into deep water, the cork handle turning increasingly vertical until it slipped below the surface. By now it was nearly dark. He peered at his expensive gold wristwatch only to discover it permanently displaying no more than the precise moment he flopped into the drink.

The next day Coop spent several fruitless hours searching along the beach for his missing wallet. It never showed up.

He did find one left shoe, though.

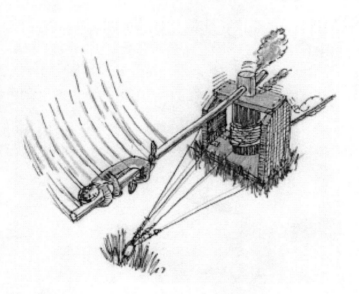

A couple of miles off the coast at Victoria in British Columbia is an idyllic island of about ten square miles named after Captain Cook's ship,

224

CHAPTER 22
CAPTAIN OF THE GOOD SHIP, CORDWOOD.

the Discovery. Half Indian Native Reserve and half provincial park, the half that is now park was once owned by Captain Beaumont and his wife who settled there during the very early days of the twentieth century.

The Beaumonts, both quite ancient by the time our paths crossed during the late thirties, were living relics of a long dead Victorian England. They had endeavored to bring with them as much pomp and ceremony as possible from "Olde Blighty" to civilize this particularly rocky corner of the new world. On Discovery Island they reigned in faded glory over their small, glimmering remnant of the "Bertish Empah".

In England, the mere hint of a Beaumont in discomfort would have brought lackeys of various shapes and sizes, panting with wide-eyed

CHAPTER 22
CAPTAIN OF THE GOOD SHIP, CORDWOOD.

deference, falling all over themselves to do their bidding. That kind of blind deference has always been a rare commodity in Canada and not likely to show up on a small island far out on the west coast. Mrs.Beaumont never became accustomed to this lack of professional. kowtowing. She often ran afoul of local residents when upon issuing an imperious command, she would be met with a snort of derision and given detailed Canadian frontier style instructions as to where she could put her demand.

Captain Beaumont, a small wiry individual with a strange bounding walk caused by an injury in his past, really needed not much looking after for he was inordinately well blessed and seems to have sailed through life accompanied by great slatherings of blind good luck as well. Mrs

CHAPTER 22
CAPTAIN OF THE GOOD SHIP, CORDWOOD.

Beaumont very seldom showed herself in public and when she did, she was always garbed in long, sombre black dresses from the turn of the century. Where Captain Beaumont was open and friendly, Mrs. B was the opposite. Cold and distant, she was the perfect picture of imperious authority. Looking a little too much like the twin sister of Toto's nemesis in the Wizard of Oz, I can tell you she kept me in a state of constant terror and gave me the creeps.

I was seven when my parents worked for the Beaumonts in the mid thirties, my father as engineer on the "Discovery Isle", the Beaumont yacht, and my mother as cook and general factotum around the Beaumont house.

The "Discovery Isle", a beautiful yacht of old world design and detailed workmanship in varnished teak and polished brass, was their primary means of transportation. Her remains lie rotting on the bottom of the ocean between Trial Island and Vancouver island.

Captain Beaumont blundered about the coast on her, testing the hardness factor of every rock and reef from Alaska to Puget Sound. The first time I ever laid eyes on the "Discovery Isle" she was in the process of being yanked off a reef inside Victoria harbour by a massive steam tug.

Captain and Mrs. Beaumont once cruised north up the inside passage and when stopping for the night, anchored close to a wharf somewhere around Alert Bay. A local native, watching the Beaumont anchoring procedure which usually became an interesting exhibition of loud and misunderstood communications, called

CHAPTER 22
CAPTAIN OF THE GOOD SHIP, CORDWOOD.

over to Captain Beaumont. In his typically soft, polite, unhurried native voice he commented that maybe it wouldn't be a very good idea to locate the Discovery Isle in that particular spot for very long. Mrs. Beaumont, hearing the exchange from below, stormed on deck and dressed the interloper down in no uncertain terms.

"My husband, the Captain, will anchor his ship where so ever he pleases and I'll thank you to mind your own business!" she snorted.

Poor Captain Beaumont, caught between local wisdom from an experienced seaman on the one hand and a permanently cantankerous harpy on the other, decided to leave the boat where it was.

Dawn found the Discovery Isle suspended several feet in the air, squatting precariously on a

229

CHAPTER 22
CAPTAIN OF THE GOOD SHIP, CORDWOOD.

clutch of rotting pilings left over from a previous wharf that were completely hidden at high tide. As there wasn't another tide high enough to refloat the Discovery Isle until twenty four hours later, the Beaumonts were subjected to a constant stream of local residents offering aid and invective and whatever else came to mind until late the following night.

My father's job on the island was to keep all the mechanical equipment on Discovery Island working properly. If the water system broke down, it was his job to get it going again. If the boat went on the fritz, he was on call. No matter what the problems might be, they invariably ended up in his lap.

Because of the awesome beauty of the island, preserving its natural amenities was always a primary consideration. This attitude meant that obtaining firewood was a constant headache. Father decided that while cutting wood by hand from storm tossed logs lying on the beach kept the indigenous trees safe, it was still one awfully tiring job to pack each block of wood up the high bank from the beach to where it could be loaded into a wheel barrow and trundled off to the woodshed.

Being highly inventive, it wasn't long before he had applied pencil to paper and designed a capstan winch which, with sufficient effort, could haul a whole log up the bank to the plateau at the top in one piece where it could be sliced up and hauled away with a considerable economy of effort. Actually, the name he applied to the device was "windlass", which was a bit of a misnomer

231

CHAPTER 22
CAPTAIN OF THE GOOD SHIP, CORDWOOD.

because "wind" was something the operator required more of, not less.

This windlass stood about four feet high and looked a lot like a giant spool had escaped from a huge sewing machine and was standing vertically with a long pole crosswise through a hole in the top providing the means whereby the spool could be rotated on its axis. The middle part of the spool had a long piece of steel cable wound around it a number of times. The machine was back stayed with cables to a log buried in the ground called a "deadman". You can understand my distress when I asked my father why he was digging the hole only to be told that he was going to bury a "deadman". I looked cautiously and carefully all about but failed to spot one.

To operate this outstanding machine, the

CHAPTER 22
CAPTAIN OF THE GOOD SHIP, CORDWOOD.

spool was unwound to allow the end of the cable to be dragged down to the beach and attached to one end of a suitable log. At this point, the pole would be inserted into the hole in the top of the spool and the operator(s), pushing on the outer end of the pole, walked around and around the spool, eventually dragging the log to the top of the bank. Hence, "windlass".

A small timber, not too waterlogged, was a convenient piece of work for one man. The bigger the log, the more sweating bodies were required. Because the logs were being grudgingly dragged up a steep chute made of smaller logs, there was sometimes considerable trouble getting everything to work together and cooperate. It often became necessary to pour water onto the chute to reduce the friction.

CHAPTER 22
CAPTAIN OF THE GOOD SHIP, CORDWOOD.

One day a particularly large log floated in on the tide. I could tell from the gleam in my father's eyes that, come hell or high water, this grandaddy of all firewood logs was going to be dragged to the top of the chute and would be cut into the best firewood the world had ever seen.

It would require that all three bodies available be put to work to turn the windlass while a constant supply of water would be needed to keep the chute slippery.

So the process began. Captain Beaumont, Vic, the hired hand and my father, all heaving the handle around in a circle. As the log started up the chute it became heavier and heavier. Soon it slowed down and stopped. Then my father would dance over and dump another bucket of water down the chute. It must have been about then

CHAPTER 22
CAPTAIN OF THE GOOD SHIP, CORDWOOD.

that he remembered that wet, green grass was also a great source of lubrication so he mixed up a soup of grass and water and stirred it thoroughly together.

By now, they had this very big log quite a few feet up the chute but it had bogged down again for the umpteenth time. Leaving the other two men holding on to the pole to maintain the gains they had made, Dad nipped smartly over to the chute and dumped in a bucket of water and grass.

The results were miraculous and instantaneous. The log, now having become a rebellious free spirit, sprang to life and shot off down the chute from whence it came. The spool immediately began to unwind at a frightening speed. Vic instantly let go of the pole and

CHAPTER 22
CAPTAIN OF THE GOOD SHIP, CORDWOOD.

dropped to the ground, no fool he, because he knew it would be returning in a second or so and going at a pretty good clip, too.

Captain Beaumont, British, y'know, never learned how to spell "surrender", failed to recognize the inherent danger and hung on to the pole with dogged determination. In fact, before the pole had made much more than a quarter of a rotation, the captain, the size of his eyes belying the determination of his chin, had his arms and legs all wound around the pole like an amorous octopus.

He was no more than a blur by the third rotation when the centrifugal forces involved finally squirted him off the end of the handle like a champagne cork and he soared expertly across the clearing, bounced once or twice before

CHAPTER 22
CAPTAIN OF THE GOOD SHIP, CORDWOOD.

disappearing off into the woods.

The windlass, never designed to rotate at a maximum speed above one or two rotations per minute, was humming and smoking and leaping up and down a couple of feet and making a noise like a helicopter trying to land in a woodpile. Fortunately, it slowed down soon after shedding the captain. Meanwhile, father had grabbed me by the back of my shirt and flung me, like a bag of garbage, over the edge of the bank. Together we hunkered down in a slightly safer location to wait out the maelstrom.

Of course, when the log reached the bottom of the chute, it stopped and shortly after, so did the whirling handle of the windlass. As silence returned, Dad poked his head up see if anyone had been killed.

CHAPTER 22
CAPTAIN OF THE GOOD SHIP, CORDWOOD.

There wasn't a soul in sight.

It wasn't long before the captain staggered from the brush looking like he'd been guest of honour at a buffalo stampede. By the look of him, he must have bounced quite a few times before finally touching down for good and skidding to a halt. Since he could think of no pressing reason to linger about at the site of his latest waterloo, he bobbed determinedly off in a straight line towards home without so much as a sidelong glance. He was grumbling to himself in a low but determined voice. I couldn't make out what he was saying but I thought I caught something about going to look for some for bandages.

Vic, whom we located some distance away in the woods by his shrieking laughter, was lying on his back behind a very large tree. He was so weak from his guffawing, he couldn't get up off the ground for several minutes.

The log, once cut into smaller pieces, was winched up the chute with no further trouble.

Father had explored and discovered not only some of his own limitations but also those of the windlass, Captain Beaumont and Vic.

And as long as there was enough firewood to keep the home fires burning and the missus happy, the Captain would never mentioned the word "firewood" again.

Nor did he ever again show up to assist on the windlass.

Some time later he did mention that using a catapult as the soldiers did in England several centuries ago to fling large rocks and dead cows and other repulsive stuff at their enemies was

239

CHAPTER 22
CAPTAIN OF THE GOOD SHIP, CORDWOOD.

not that much different from how he had been

flung a half mile back into the woods.

CHAPTER 23
JUST ONE MORE DAY AT THE GRIND.

It was the sort of goofy, possibly even insane caper that, indulged in today, would surely lodge both the participants in the crow bar hotel for several birthdays.

The ingredients? A dark blue 1946 Ford sedan, some dynamite and a couple of eager, inventive nitwits always on the look out for an easier way to the job.

The Ford was in our auto body shop because it had acquired a large, shallow dent in its trunk lid, a clean, symmetrical injury without gouge or crease. The paint wasn't even scratched.

To a couple of resourceful chaps like us, it appeared that there should some simple way to remove the dent quickly and easily. If we could come up with a new and more effective method to restore the original appearance without having to go through all the normal rigamarole like filing, priming and sanding and spraying etc., we could very well retire on our earnings. For instance, if it were possible to apply air pressure evenly over the inside of the lid, the dent would pop out like

242

the bottom of an oil can.

Had the Ford been reasonably air tight, this treatment might have been possible by inflating the trunk like a balloon, but every old Ford of my acquaintance was about as airtight as a screen door.

The fellow on the job with me was supposed to be my boss but we were more like partners. We did most things by consensus and while in this state of fraternal geniality we concluded that the required amount of air pressure could probably be generated by a carefully controlled explosion. Probably a half stick of slow speed Dynamite called "stumping powder" would do it.

We briefly considered the possibility of applying this explosive force to the trunk lid while

243

still bolted in place on the car. However, in one of those rare moments this consideration was overtaken by uncharacteristic sanity, we decided against that approach. Should we have miscalculated, I was sure that the side effects would have been enormously difficult to explain to the surprised owner of what ever was left of his car.

It took no time to round up a stick of stumping powder, some fuse and a blasting cap. We unbolted the trunk lid and hauled it to the gravel parking lot hind the community hall.

We then laid part of the stick of dynamite on the ground with the fuse and cap in place, situated the lid squarely over it, weighted it down with a half a dozen handy railway ties, lit the fuse and giggling like a couple of schoolgirls, retired briskly to the other side of the hall.

We expected a reasonable "WHUMP" or a healthy "BANG" but the puny, anemic "SNAP" like a Halloween firecracker was a genuine disappointment. We cautiously sidled up to the blast site to find that the cap had exploded but had failed to detonate the powder. Damp! We repeated the routine with the rest of the stick with identical results.

Foray time! We returned to our suspicious supplier and quickly obtained more stumping powder and after a couple of hours of lighting fuses and haring off into the woods, we'd used up maybe eight blasting caps, twenty feet of fuse, several sticks of powder and still no bang. All of the dynamite we had obtained was damp and obviously had no intention of living up to its

245

CHAPTER 23
JUST ONE MORE DAY AT THE GRIND.

infamous reputation.

After more scrounging, we talked a neighbour out of one stick of 85 per cent rock powder. Because dynamite for blasting rock is only slightly less volatile than a hive full of hungry hornets, we decided to use less than a quarter stick. Didn't want to take a chance on doing any serious damage, y'see.

We'd forgotten that, splattered around under that trunk lid, was a very large supply of unexploded dynamite craftily relaxing with its eyes closed, pretending to be asleep. Guess what happened.

That chunk of 85 per cent, very macho rock powder was the perfect alarm clock to awaken all that dormant dynamite.

Again, one of us lit the fuse and we

galloped off to hide behind the Hall. We were astounded by the paralyzing "KABOOM" that rattled miles of countryside as all that accumulated dynamite flexed its muscles and went roaring off to work in one great, shattering explosion.

We stared at each other in shock while being

hosed with a hail of leaves and gravel and general debris. Out of the corner of my eye, I spotted a large torn chunk of dark blue Ford trunk lid several hundred feet above us being chased by a thinning plume of dust, dirt and rocks. Spinning like a top, it rapidly gained altitude and flapped resolutely off in a southerly direction like a migrating goose.

The parking lot looked like down town Halifax after the explosion and was swathed in

247

CHAPTER 23
JUST ONE MORE DAY AT THE GRIND.

drifting layers of acrid smoke. Where the lid had been was a crater big enough to entomb a Volkswagen bus. The timbers were broken and split and lying all over the place like a bunch of unconscious drunks after a bar room brawl.

Not only did we have to spring for a new trunk lid but it cost us one very large truckload of gravel to fill the hole. Three, if you count what we had to pay the trucker to acquire a sudden case of amnesia.

And twenty one window panes in the hall at a buck each.

But there's still nothing as soul satisfying as a real loud, rollicking explosion complete with great clouds of dust and flying debris..

CHAPTER 24
MY FAVOURITE TIME OF THE YEAR

SPRING

Spring is sprung, the grass is riz,
I wonder where the boidies is?
Some say the boid is on the wing,
But that's absoid, the wing is on the
boid.

AUTHOR UNKNOWN BUT GREATLY APPRECIATED

Spring: that time of year when women finally think about what men think about all the time.

The massive, towering snow banks lodged high in the mountains begin their slow, steady melt down. Sluiced away by the annual increased flow of water hurrying to the sea, the milky chemical soup eroded from the mountains stony surfaces by winter's frosts is carried into

CHAPTER 24
MY FAVOURITE TIME OF THE YEAR

lakes and oceans. Occasionally, uncontrolled flooding deposits this soup as a grey, mucky layer evenly coating the plains, the forests and sometimes, even the cities and homes as the melt water slowly recedes.

Without this annual ritual, there could be no life as we know it.

The Egyptians recognized the benefit of this phenomena more than 5000 years ago and artfully adapted their farming procedures. Every year the flooding Nile not only revitalized and rejuvenated and fertilized the land but also inconveniently washed away all the survey stakes. As soon as the water receded, the Pharaoh's surveyors would spread out across the land to officially re define the boundaries before the farmers had time to fight about it. Probably arising from this significant annual ritual came the observance practiced by so many of the world's religions to use immersion in water as being symbolic of a new start, a renewal of purpose, a cleansing, one's personal spring or, to be born again.

A clever fellow named Noah, despite the derisive snorts and chuckles of his neighbours, built a large wooden boat, an Ark, a container of valuables, and thus survived one of those floods, while thoughtfully preserving those animals likely to be required by mankind after the flood was over. The rest of the world was scoured clean, ready for a new start.

One Thursday - about three thousand years

ago an unidentified Roman official noticed that he had enjoyed a particularly happy and beneficial day. The only thing about his routine he'd done any differently was that for breakfast he'd eaten a hard boiled egg that had been dipped in cold salt water.

"Mandatum" he cried wisely, which is Latin for a "A New Commandment". After due consideration he decided the new commandant would be "Love one another!" Probably not the first time nor the last that a really hard boiled egg or two bound some chap over into cause for serious contemplation.

Today, in a typically confusing English manner, we have named this Thursday - Maunday; having shortened Mandatum Thursday

252

CHAPTER 24
MY FAVOURITE TIME OF THE YEAR

to Maunday-Thursday and now we create Holy Easter Eggs by boiling the Hell out of them on Maunday - Thursday - which explains why once year everybody goes around looking confused, asking, "When is Easter this year, on Maundy or - Thursday - or is it Sunday?"

Whoever enters their opinion first wins!

In Latin, PASCHA, the origin of the Hebrew PESACH, or PASSOVER reminds the Jews of their escape from bondage in Egypt and is brought to full focus each year on Seder Night. Unleavened bread, wine and bitter herbs help to concentrate their commemoration.

One religious group, after considerable rumination, decided that the sun, was in fact, a God whom they named Adonis or Attis; he who dies each winter and is reborn each spring. In the manner of all religious groups, there were the rebels. This disgruntled group, the Saxons, after due and serious consideration, decided that the sun was actually a woman, a female, a goddess named Eostre from which we derive the name Easter.

The Egyptians dreamed up the majestic pageantry of the legend of the Phoenix while Mistletoe has been for thousands of generations a symbol of everlasting life as well as being considered a traditionally adequate excuse for the occasional Yule time grope.

Hindus celebrate HOLI, the day to contemplate an ancient legend of a Prince who escaped the clutches of the wicked Goddess

"HOLIKA". They light bonfires to drive away the darkness of winter and smear themselves with ashes and red dye.

Sikhs enjoy HOLA MAHALLAH on a New Years Day that falls on our April 13.

Orientals support April's CH'ING MING or Day of Pure Brightness.

The Buddhist's day of renewal is April 8th.

And so it goes. April Fools Day. Arbour Day. Morris Dancing. Kentucky Derby. Skipping. Marbles. And the opening of the Salmon Season. How could any other time even remotely compare with this brightest, cleanest, newest of all seasons.

Prepared for winter storage in countless different ways, last years seeds lie dormant,

CHAPTER 24
MY FAVOURITE TIME OF THE YEAR

waiting for renewal. Some, to grow well, first require being frozen for a time during the winter. Others need to feel the presence of free ions rising from the soil. But all respond to the sun's warming rays of early spring. Swelling, imperceptively at first, cells divide and divide yet again, becoming roots and becoming stems and becoming leaves in a process unchanged over millions of years.

In a cave hollowed out under the roots of a huge Red Cedar, a she bear and her cubs respond to that invisible part of the sun's spectrum that holds the power to penetrate through the soil into her den. The cubs, now several weeks old, create a sense of urgency that she, like most mothers, must arise and do

CHAPTER 24
MY FAVOURITE TIME OF THE YEAR

something about breakfast for the youngsters.

Close by, listening to her instinctive urging and concealing herself in a sun dappled thicket of Spirea on a bed of dead leaves, a Whitetail doe has reached her full term. In moments, she's licking the delicate, spotted miniature clone of herself as it stands on wobbly legs and starts to suckle.

In any one of hundreds of small valleys and river deltas suspended between towering mountain ranges, the last of the snow quietly trickles away from the shadows under the trees on the northern end of the clearings. At the end of the vale, near a creek, is a small house, a few out buildings and a pole and shake barn. Inside the barn a farmer watches the swallows building mud nests in the eaves as he starts preparing his machinery for the season's production. He works his way through a list tacked up on the wall, a summary written over the past winter as he noticed the various things that would require doing. The plough, its moulding board, thoroughly greased the previous year at the end of the season, was ready to use. Not so the seed drill. Oats left in the chutes had become damp, germinated and grown, clogging the whole system. The baler needs cleaning and adjusting. The old hay, removed from the barn to make room for the new crop, will be stored and used for bedding. The new hay crop of rich grasses and wild flowers is well into this years growth. By the middle of May it could be ready to be cut, tedded,

CHAPTER 24
MY FAVOURITE TIME OF THE YEAR

raked and baled.

From everywhere, in the trees, in the bushes, in the grass rises the hum of bees getting on with the business of making honey. They are surely unaware of it but without bees, few plants could survive to go forward with renewal. And nor would I survive without a dollop of honey for my breakfast toast. Bees trundle from flower to flower, busily gathering ripest pollen from which they manufacture food for their next generation. While at it, they inadvertently carry the pollen from one plant to another, enabling more renewal.

Small children sitting in school classrooms, look through the windows and watch spring arrive. They drive their teachers nuts with their fidgeting and fussing. The buzzer sounds their release and they pour into the school yard to play marbles, hop scotch and skipping and many more which I have no way of interpreting.

Down at the sea shore, brightly plumed drakes each rush about corralling a personal harem to be segregated and protected from interlopers. Swooping like fighting aircraft or rushing belligerently after one another like feathered speedboats, they duke it out with all the determination and bravado of rutting moose, winner take all, no quarter given or asked.

High above, long skeins of geese steer their instinctive course across the warming sky, inexorably drawn to the swamps and bayous of the north country. With a little luck in a few

CHAPTER 24
MY FAVOURITE TIME OF THE YEAR

weeks they will be herding flocks of goslings between low islands, freshly green with new reeds and grasses.

In a fleeting moment, just when we are really getting into enjoying it and remembering how wonderful it is, Spring flies on silent wings and is gone. One morning we look out the window and it's over, finished and has been replaced by the long hot days of summer.

ISBN 155212790-7